The Polyvagal Theory

A Complete Self-Help Guide to Understanding the Autonomic Nervous System for Accessing the Healing Power of the Vagus Nerve - Learn to Manage Anxiety, Depression, Trauma and Autism

Table of Contents

Introduction *7*

Chapter One: Introduction to the Autonomic Nervous System *10*

Chapter Two: Autonomic Nervous System and Introduction to the Polyvagal Theory *28*

Chapter Three: Stephen Porges' Polyvagal Theory *49*

Chapter Four: Stanley Rosenberg's Polyvagal Theory ... *67*

Chapter Five: Practical Guide to Applying the Polyvagal Theory *85*

Chapter Six: Using the Polyvagal Theory as a Counselor *103*

Conclusion *119*

Introduction

In the world which we live today, troubles abound. From trauma to various levels of depression, it is clear that the world is plagued by many ailments. While this is undeniably true, there are some trusted methods with which people can address these problems.

When it comes to managing issues such as anxiety and stress, a number of methods come to mind. However, the polyvagal theory which was expounded by Stephen Porges and Stanley Rosenberg would turn out to be one of the best guides available.

This book will thus focus on these theories and provide many keys and tools from which to choose. Some of these will include:

- Learning the various parts of the autonomic nervous system and how they influence certain reactions

- Understanding the various reactions humans are prone to when faced with various challenging circumstances

- Learning how the polyvagal theory helps to make life easier

- Learning how the polyvagal theory can be applied in your life or as a counselor

- Understanding how the polyvagal theory affects the management of autism and stress in general.

By the end of this book, you should have a well-rounded understanding of the polyvagal theory and will be able to effectively apply it, thereby improving your life.

Chapter One: Introduction to the Autonomic Nervous System

Have you been facing chronic feelings of anxiety?

Have you been fighting depressive feelings, wondering whether everything will be alright?

I understand.

Statistics have shown that some of the highest causes of death in the world are anxiety, depression and feelings of boredom and loneliness. And why wouldn't they be? Our world has become one of survival of the fittest. People wake up in the morning with countless activities lined up for the day that often consume the time meant for resting and self-reflection. We go to our jobs and work hard until late in the evening and sometimes head to other events before going home for the night. High school and post-secondary students are daily loaded up with work on top of domestic responsibilities to home, family members and friends.

Technology, despite the numerous benefits it adds to society and the ease with which it helps us carry out our work, has made certain things more difficult. We behold the glamorous lifestyles of celebrities and we feel that our lives are like a puzzle that's missing pieces. We scroll through social media and see friends and strangers alike having the time of their lives while we lay in bed, thinking of what to squeeze out for a meal. Most times we tend to ignore it, but accumulated depressive feelings combined with everyday stress can leave us feeling that there is something wrong with our lives.

But there isn't. Snap out of it!

The first step to getting out of a situation is to UNDERSTAND it. It is understanding the problem that helps you adjust your attitude toward certain situations and solve the problem appropriately. In this case, the source is one of your body systems.

So what is one of the most important systems to note in the body? The autonomic nervous system.

What Is the Autonomic Nervous System?

Certainly, you are familiar with the term 'nervous system'. It is a complex part of the body that is responsible for automatically coordinating the body's actions and sensory information by sending signals from one part of the body to another. It performs this task through a special type of cell called a neuron or a nerve cell.

The nervous system consists of two main parts: the central

nervous system (CNS) and the peripheral nervous system (PNS). The CNS is made up of the brain and spinal cord, the importance of which is obvious. The brain controls all body functions including movement, awareness, thought, speech, memory, and much more. The spinal cord is linked to a portion of the brain called the brainstem where it sends messages from the brain to the peripheral nerves and vice versa, and it also plays a very vital role in body positioning.

The peripheral nervous system can be said to oversee all activities which take place in the body apart from the brain and spinal cord, or the CNS. Its primary role is to ensure that the various body parts are communicating well and working in harmony. When communication is at its peak, we will be able to react appropriately to the various stimuli we sense from the environment.

You are probably asking yourself where the autonomic nervous system fits into all of this.

Relax... stay with me. You will soon find out.

The peripheral nervous system is further divided into two parts: the somatic nervous system and the autonomic nervous system (ANS).

Aha... Now we're talking...

The word 'somatic' is derived from the Greek word 'soma' which means 'body'. This implies that the somatic nervous system is responsible for sending and receiving motor and sensory information either to or from the CNS. It is also a major player in voluntary movement. To this effect, this system consists of two major types of neurons –sensory and motor neurons–which carry information from the body to the brain and spinal cord, and from the brain and spinal cord to the body, respectively. It is their actions that result in a response to physical stimuli.

Finally, there is the autonomic nervous system. The ANS is otherwise called the vegetative nervous system. It is the part of the peripheral nervous system that directly controls the function of internal organs such as glands, blood vessels, genitals, lungs, heart, smooth muscles, etc. This system carries out activities in the body unconsciously or without thought such as respiration, heart rate, urination, digestion, and sexual arousal, for example. It is also in charge of the fight-flight-freeze response. This theory was first discovered by the intellectual Walter Cannon.

The ANS is controlled by the hypothalamus in the brain. This means that the hypothalamus controls autonomic or automatic functions such as breathing, heartbeat and reflexes such as sneezing, vomiting and coughing. These functions are still subdivided into different areas and linked to subsystems of the ANS. The hypothalamus, which is located just a bit above the brain stem, integrates these autonomic functions. This system is one of the most important systems in the human body as any disorder of this system may be progressive or irreversible and can affect the entire body.

Now the ANS is divided into three systems: the sympathetic nervous system, the parasympathetic nervous system and the enteric nervous system, but the major systems are the first two. The enteric nervous system hasn't yet been globally recognized as part of the ANS, and some textbooks do not even include it. Therefore, we will start with the first two.

The Sympathetic Nervous System

What is the sympathetic nervous system?

Think about past or current fears. Whether we admit it or not, most of us have fears, whether mild or extreme. The way you respond to fear is known as the fight-flight-freeze response (or acute stress response). This response is controlled and managed by the sympathetic nervous system. It is usually active at a low level to regulate homeostasis, which is equilibrium and harmony in the body.

Interesting, isn't it? So how does it work?

Sympathetic nerves begin in the central nervous system in the sections of the spine known as the thoracic spine and the lumbar spine. It is sometimes referred to as the thoracolumbar outflow because the axons or ends of these cells exit the spine here and communicate or synapse with either sympathetic ganglion cells (which connect to and regulate various organs including the heart) or specialized cells in the kidneys and the adrenal glands (which sit on top of the kidneys).

Sympathetic neurons emit neurotransmitters or chemicals called epinephrine and norepinephrine (also known as adrenaline and noradrenaline). Adrenaline, as we know, jumpstarts the body into action, with effects such as increasing heart rate, diverting blood flow from the organs toward the skeletal muscles, dilating pupils and increasing sweating, for example.

Sympathetic nerves that connect to the kidneys release a chemical called dopamine. Dopamine can be turned into norepinephrine (noradrenaline) in the adrenal glands if the body signals for it. Sympathetic nerves that connect to chromaffin cells in the adrenal glands produce substantial amounts of epinephrine (adrenaline) from norepinephrine). Both epinephrine and norepinephrine result in responses that ready the body for action under stress.

Why is this system known as the 'sympathetic' nervous system, of all things? History has it that this name stems from the idea of sympathy. Sympathy is the perception of someone's or something's distress and reacting accordingly, so it was thought of in the sense of having a connection between parts or people. It was first used medically by Claudius Galenus (otherwise known as Galen of Pergamon). But in the 18th century, it was used specifically for nerves by French anatomist, Jacob B. Winslow.

Now we will address the second part of the autonomic nervous system.

The Parasympathetic Nervous System

The autonomic nervous system regulates the unconscious actions of the body, and the parasympathetic nervous system (PSNS) controls the unconscious activities that take place when the body is at rest, often after eating. These activities include salivation, lacrimation (tear flow), sexual arousal, digestion, urination, defecation, etc. and they are often known as 'feed and breed' or 'rest and digest' activities. The function of the PSNS complements that of the sympathetic nervous system, which regulates fight-flight-freeze responses.

Parasympathetic nerves have a craniosacral outflow (they exit the CNS from the brain stem or from the sacral region of the spine), compared to the sympathetic system that has a thoracolumbar outflow.

So what is the structure of this system?

The nerves in this system are autonomic, and their supply primarily stems from these three sources: the cranial nerves, the vagus nerve and the pelvic splanchnic nerves.

Parasympathetic nerves (a special type of cranial nerve) stem from particular nuclei (groups of nerve cells in the CNS) and form a synapse at any of the four parasympathetic ganglia (groups of nerve cells outside the CNS or in the PNS). It is from there that these nerves reach their target tissues through trigeminal nerves (nerves that are responsible for motor and sensory functions). Another type of cranial nerve is called the oculomotor nerve, which regulates most of the eye-related parasympathetic functions.

The vagus nerve originates in the lower half of the brain stem which is connected to the spinal cord (known as the brain stem medulla). The term 'vagus nerve' originates from the Latin word 'vagus' which means 'wandering'. This is appropriate considering that this nerve controls a lot of target tissues. However, the vagus nerve is quite unusual because it doesn't follow the trigeminal nerve path to get to its destination (the target tissues). Also, this nerve is very difficult to trace because it is virtually everywhere in the thorax and abdomen. As such, several parasympathetic nerves leave the vagus nerve as they enter the thorax, such as the laryngeal and cardiac nerves. The organs affected by the parasympathetic nerves in the abdomen include the pancreas, kidney and gall bladder among others.

The pelvic splanchnic nerves exit the spine through the sacral region. They contribute immensely to the supply of nerves to the genital and pelvic organs. They regulate urinary excretion, the sensation of pain, and sexual functions like penis erection.

Remember when it was stated that the parasympathetic nervous system has a *cranio-sacral* outflow? The pelvic splanchnic nerves are an important *sacral* component of the PSNS. It is in the same location as the sacral splanchnic nerves that emerge from the sympathetic trunk in the SNS.

Parasympathetic nerves produce the neurotransmitter acetylcholine, which is received by the target organs which respond by stimulating parasympathetic activities.

Relationship Between the Sympathetic and Parasympathetic Nervous Systems

The interesting thing about the sympathetic and parasympathetic components of the autonomic nervous system is that they work opposite each other. First, the SNS controls actions that require quick and immediate response while the PSNS controls slower or delayed activities. Furthermore, the SNS speeds up the body processes, for example, increasing the heart rate when faced with imminent danger. The PSNS on the other hand calms the body, for example reducing heart rate.

Muscles stimulated by the SNS contract while those stimulated by the PSNS relax. The SNS releases adrenaline while the PSNS has no connection with the adrenal gland. The same goes for glycogen conversion; the SNS transforms glycogen into glucose for muscle energy. The bronchial tubes constrict when influenced by the PSNS but dilate under the influence of the SNS. There is an increase in urinary output when the PSNS is active, while the opposite happens with SNS activity. The neurons in the PSNS are cholinergic (produce and receive acetylcholine), while in the SNS neurons are adrenergic (produce and receive norepinephrine/epinephrine).

The Enteric Nervous System (ENS)

Otherwise known as the intrinsic nervous system, the ENS is one of the systems in the ANS. Its system of neurons in the lining of the gastrointestinal tract regulate the activities of the GI tract from the esophagus all the way down to the anus. One powerful thing about this system is that it can work without the sympathetic and parasympathetic systems but may be affected by them. The ENS, also more trendily known as the gut, is sometimes referred to as the second brain.

This system operates without the brain and the spinal cord but needs the supply of nerves from the autonomic nervous system through the prevertebral ganglia and vagus nerve. However, research has shown that the enteric nervous system can function even with a severed vagus nerve. The neurons from this system not only secrete enzymes from the gastrointestinal tract but also regulate motor functions.

The ENS contains over 500 million neurons. There are over 100 million neurons in the spinal cord alone. These neurons interact via neurotransmitters that are almost the same as those used in the CNS, and they include dopamine, serotonin and acetylcholine.

The Function of the Autonomic Nervous System in the Body

Recall that the autonomic nervous system is a division of the peripheral nervous system, which is a division of the nervous system as a whole. The ANS is responsible for regulating functions that are carried out without conscious effort. Then it was also stated that the ANS has two divisions–the sympathetic nervous system (SNS) and the parasympathetic nervous system (PSNS).

It would therefore be fitting to say that the functions of the ANS are the functions of the individual divisions. The SNS takes care of fight-or-flight responses. The PSNS takes care of the actions the body undertakes at rest, especially after eating. The ENS takes care of the activities of the gastrointestinal tract.

So what exactly are the functions of these systems?

Functions of the Sympathetic Nervous System

1.   It regulates homeostasis. This function does not just apply to human beings but to all living organisms. The fibers in this system supply nerves to the tissues of almost every organ in the body. This process regulates diverse functions like blood flow, urinary control, pupil dilation and constriction, body temperature, blood sugar levels, pH, etc.

2.   It regulates the fight-or-flight response, sometimes called fight-flight-freeze response or the sympathoadrenal response (derived from the words 'sympathetic' and 'adrenal medulla'). This is one of the most important functions of the SNS. It controls the hormonal and neuronal stress response in a way that the preganglionic fibers in the system activate the release of epinephrine (adrenaline) in great quantities, acting directly on the cardiovascular system. When activated, the SNS or fight-or-flight response:

•   Constricts blood vessels, especially those in the kidney and skin. This happens when the adrenergic receptors are activated by norepinephrine that is released by postganglionic neurons. This also causes a redirection of blood flow from the skin and gastrointestinal tract.

• Boosts blood flow to the lungs and skeletal muscles.

• Allows the coronary vessels of the heart to widen or relax, especially the ones in large arteries, large veins and smaller arterioles.

• Prevents peristalsis, thereby preventing digestion.

3. It gets the body ready for action, especially in life-threatening situations. For instance, the SNS prepares your body in the morning before you wake up by increasing its outflow spontaneously.

4. It relaxes the ciliary muscles in the eye linked to the lens and dilates pupils, thereby allowing more light to penetrate the eye.

5. It dilates the bronchioles of the lungs by spreading epinephrine continuously, thereby improving oxygen exchange.

6. It increases heart rate. The contribution of both the sympathetic and parasympathetic nervous systems to the sinoatrial node regulates heart rate. Note that heart rate is different from heart rhythm. Heart rate is the number of times the heart beats per second, while the heart rhythm is the pattern in which the heart beats. When heart rate is

increased, blood flow to the heart and active skeletal muscles is improved.

7.   It stimulates sweat excretion in sweat glands.

8.   It prevents tumescence or swelling. Penis tumescence is commonly known as penis erection which entails blood filling the penis in preparation for sexual activity. When faced with life-threatening situations, the SNS prevents this from occurring.

9.   It constricts all intestinal and urinary sphincters.

10.   It activates orgasm.

Functions of the Parasympathetic Nervous System

Recall that the parasympathetic nervous system functions directly opposite to the sympathetic nervous system. The PSNS:

1. Aids sexual activity. The nerves in this system help to erect the genital tissues through the pelvic splanchnic nerves. When a man is about to ejaculate, the sympathetic system causes the internal pelvic sphincter to close and the urethral muscle to undergo peristalsis. Likewise, the parasympathetic system causes peristalsis to occur in the urethral muscle, and the bulbospongiosus muscles are contracted by the

pudendal nerve to violently discharge the semen. The penis becomes flaccid again afterward.

2. Increases blood flow by relaxing or widening blood vessels that are linked to the gastrointestinal tract.

3. Enhances near vision by contracting the pupil and constricting the ciliary muscles in the eye. This is the exact opposite of what the SNS does, which is enhance far vision.

4. Improves absorption of nutrients by enhancing the secretion of saliva and the rate of peristalsis.

5. Reduces the diameter of the bronchioles when the body needs less oxygen.

6. Lowers heart rate, by producing acetylcholine, contrary to the sympathetic nervous system which increases heart rate by producing epinephrine and norepinephrine (or adrenaline and noradrenaline).

Functions of the Enteric Nervous System

The ENS (also known as the second brain) has its own unique function since it is the nervous system that coordinates the processes of the gastrointestinal system. The ENS:

1. Acts as a neuron integrating unit. This system is called the second brain primarily because it can exist

on its own. It interacts with the CNS through the prevertebral ganglia and the vagus nerve, but it can still function autonomously when the vagus nerve is severed.

Because this system is made up of several kinds of neurons (neurons that both send and receive signals), it can stand in for the CNS input as an integrating unit. These neurons act on chemical and mechanical conditions.

2. Controls GI tract secretions. Gastrointestinal enzymes are controlled by cholinergic neurons that are located on the walls of the digestive tract.

Conclusion

So there you have it! In this chapter, we understood that the nervous system is comprised of two parts–the central nervous system (CNS) and the peripheral nervous system (PNS). The PNS is further divided into the somatic nervous system and the autonomic nervous system (ANS). The ANS controls the body's unconscious functions and is divided into three–the sympathetic (SNS), the parasympathetic (PSNS) and the enteric (ENS) nervous systems.

We learned that the SNS controls the body's fight-or-flight responses by altering bodily functions. It is responsible for maintaining homeostatic processes in the body. The PSNS regulates the body's activities at rest. These activities may include salivation, lacrimation, sexual arousal/urges, digestion, etc. It is important to note that these two systems work opposite each other, yet hand in hand.

We learned that the ENS coordinates the mechanisms of the gastrointestinal tract. It regulates gastrointestinal enzymes, allows peristalsis to take place, and coordinates reflexes.

So why is knowledge of the autonomic nervous system important? To understand the way our body operates, we need to understand the systems that fuel them. We need to understand how our visceral experiences and thoughts are tied to our body systems, and one of the surest ways to do that is by understanding the polyvagal theory.

Want to know more?

Keep reading...

"Enjoying this book?

Please leave a review because we would love to hear your feedback, opinions and advice to create better products and services for you! Thank you for your support. You are greatly appreciated!"

Chapter Two: Autonomic Nervous System and Introduction to the Polyvagal Theory

The autonomic nervous system is an inherent part of the human body. It regulates and monitors the activities of most visceral organs and some skeletal muscles. The autonomic system is said to be responsible for the rest-and- digest state and the fight-or-flight response in animals. These states of the autonomic nervous system have been closely associated with the activities of the nerve known as the vagus (pneumogastric) nerve. Among the twelve cranial nerves, the vagus nerve is the tenth It is the longest nerve of the autonomic nervous system. It goes through the neck, thoracic region and abdomen. The vagus nerve has the largest distribution in the body. The vagus nerve has both sensory and motor functions. Its sensory functions are further divided into visceral and somatic components. Its visceral components innervate the internal organs of the body such as the larynx, pharynx, trachea, esophagus, lungs, heart, and the gastrointestinal tract (which has its terminal branches) while its sensory components innervate the skin on the external ear and the external auditory canal.

The fibers responsible for its motor functions innervate basically all the organs from the neck to the colon via parasympathetic fibers with the exception of the adrenal glands. Hence, the vagus nerve is responsible for peristalsis in the gastrointestinal tract, heart rate, sweating and speech. During stress, the vagus nerve is excessively activated. This is due to the strong sympathetic response that is often associated with stress resulting from overcompensation of the parasympathetic nerves. This can lead to vasovagal syncope (fainting) resulting from an abrupt decrease in cardiac output and therefore reduced blood flow to the brain. Vasovagal syncope is common in women and children. Under instances of intense fear, there might be a temporary loss of bladder control.

Introduction to the Polyvagal Theory

The polyvagal theory ensures an understanding of the diverse capacities of the medullary source (the brain stem medulla) which makes up the vagus nerve This theory identifies two functionally unique branches of the vagus nerve. These are usually divided or classified into two groups: the nucleus ambiguus (NA) and the dorsal motor nuclei (DMNX). The polyvagal theory helps to point out the connectivity between visceral activity and the nerve's parasympathetic coordination of various organs including the lungs, heart and gastrointestinal tract.

Before the advent of the polyvagal theory, it was believed that the nervous system was a two-part antagonistic system. The polyvagal theory recognizes a third response of the nervous system which is referred to as the social engagement system.

Stephen Porges' Theory

Stephen Porges is a professor of psychiatry. He is currently at North Carolina University. At Indiana University where he established the traumatic stress research consortium, he is regarded as a distinguished university scientist. He is popularly known for developing the polyvagal theory, which depicts how visceral occurrences affect the nervous system and our ensuing behavior.

The polyvagal theory introduces a new perspective that connects autonomic function to behavior. This viewpoint seeks to recognize the autonomic system as a major body system in its own right. It considers the neural circuits which then translates into autonomic reactivity as adaptive within the context of the phylogeny (evolutionary history) of the mammalian autonomic nervous system. The theory proposed a comprehensive conceptualization of the autonomic nervous system to include target organ, afferent and efferent pathways (nerves that send messages from the body to the brain, and from the brain to the body, respectively), and a pursuit to comprehend the bidirectional communication and mutual effects between the heart and the central nervous system. It analyzes paradigms, justifications, and conclusions concerning the role the autonomic system plays in the regulation of social behavior. The polyvagal theory is not static; therefore, as the knowledge of neurophysiology advances, testable hypotheses will remold and broaden the theory.

The polyvagal theory places emphasis on the phylogenetic origins of brain structures regulating adaptive survival-oriented behaviors as well as social behavior. It recognizes a hierarchy of responses that are built into the autonomic nervous system and attached to the evolution of the vertebrate animals. This evolutionary development of the mammalian autonomic system gives the neurophysiological substrates necessary for emotional responses and affective processes which are primary elements of social behavior. The theory suggests that the physiological state determines the spectrum of behavior and various experiences that are psychological in nature.

It explains emotional, social, and communication behaviors and disorders. It also provides a reasonable explanation of stress-related responses. The theory provides a clear distinction between the two branches of the vagus nerve physiologically and anatomically. It proposes that each branch of the vagus nerve can be correlated with a distinct adaptive behavioral strategy. The theory enunciates three phylogenetic stages in the evolution of the mammalian autonomic nervous system. These stages of evolution reveal the emergence of three unique subsystems that are ordered phylogenetically and behaviorally correlated with communication (vocalization, facial expression, etc.), mobilization (such as fight-or-flight response) and immobilization (syncope and behavioral shutdown).

The first to develop was the parasympathetic branch (the dorsal vagal pathway) which gives the immobilization response. It is the oldest and most primitive pathway. This pathway depends mostly on the vegetative or unmyelinated vagus nerve. The next to develop was the sympathetic branch which is responsible for mobilization response. Thirdly, the ventral vagal pathway of the parasympathetic branch is a recent addition. It carries patterns of behavioral, social and communication engagement that are unique to mammalian species.

In summary, the phylogenetic order of the autonomic nervous system can be classified as follows:

1. the dorsal vagal complex (DVC), which is the immobilization system

2. the sympathetic nervous system (SNS), which is the mobilization system supporting the fight-or-flight response

3. the ventral vagal complex (VVC), which is the mammalian signaling system responsible for motion, emotion, and communication.

Each of these subsystems makes use of strategies unique to that subsystem.

The Dorsal Vagal Complex

The dorsal vagal complex (DVC) is predominantly associated with the taste, digestive and hypoxic responses in mammals. The efferent nerve fibers for the DVC have their origin at the dorsal motor nucleus (DMNX) of the vagus nerve while its primary vagal afferent fibers terminate at the nucleus of the solitary tract, a bundle of nerve fibers in the brain stem. The function of the DVC is almost vestigial in humans. It is often triggered by hypoxia or reduced oxygen. Though this can be adaptive for reptiles, it is, however, deadly in mammals. Under physiological conditions, the DVC regulates tone of the gut and promote digestive processes. However, the DVC might play a role in pathophysiological conditions like ulcers especially when it has been up-regulated. The DVC is regarded as a last resort. When all other subsystems fail and we seem trapped, it dissociates, collapses and shuts down the autonomic nervous system.

The Sympathetic Nervous System

The sympathetic nervous system (SNS) gets the body ready for emergency situations, inhibiting activities of the gastrointestinal tract and increasing cardiac output, breathing rate and stimulating the sweat glands for protection and lubrication of the skin. The sympathetic nervous system has often been associated with stress and emotion.

The Ventral Vagal Complex

The ventral vagal complex (VVC) is the most recent development of the phylogenetic order. It primarily consists of a somatomotor component and a visceromotor component. Its primary efferent fibers originate in the nucleus ambiguus while its primary afferent fibers terminate in the source nuclei of the facial and trigeminal nerves. The vagal pathway from the nucleus ambiguus to the sinoatrial node of the heart and the bronchi are myelinated or insulated with a sheath for more efficient nerve signal transmission. The somatomotor element of the VVC contributes to the regulation and modulation of behaviors necessary for exploring the social environment. The visceromotor element of the VVC regulates vagal control of the heart and bronchi which provides metabolic resources in a social setting.

Stanley Rosenberg's Theory

Stanley Rosenberg is an author and a body therapist. He was born in America. He has been a Rolfer since 1983 and has also been a practicing craniofacial therapist since 1987. He was a student of Alain Gehin where he studied biomechanical radiotherapy for several years. He studied craniosacral therapy at the Upledger Institute. Rosenberg also took some courses in osteopathy where he was a student of Jean-Pierre Barral. For a number of years, he led a school in Denmark where he taught structural integration, scar tissue release, myofascial release, biomechanical craniosacral therapy, biotensegrity and visceral massage. Additionally, he is a yoga instructor, acrobatics instructor and voice trainer.

Stanley Rosenberg applies the healing capability of the polyvagal theory in the treatment of health conditions such as:

• Chronic obstructive pulmonary disease (COPD) and hiatal hernias

• Shoulder, neck and head pain

• Migraine headaches

• Bipolar disorder

• Post-traumatic stress disorder (PTSD)

- Anxiety and panic attacks

COPD and Hiatal Hernias

Chronic obstructive pulmonary disease is one of the most common non-communicable diseases present in the world today. Symptoms of COPD include shortness of breath, poor airflow and coughing. COPD can be caused by smoking or exposure to environmental toxins as the body reacts by laying down excess fibers in the bronchioles and lungs, narrowing the airways over time and causing breathing difficulties. Steroids and inhalers can be used to open up the airways although the symptoms are likely to return once the effect of the drug wears off.

Rosenberg is of the belief that most of the underlying problems associated with COPD arise from the dysfunction of the autonomic nervous system and can be properly addressed with the knowledge acquired from the polyvagal theory. One of the major components of his treatment of COPD is the restoration of the function of the vagus nerve.

A hiatal hernia occurs when the stomach is pulled up against the diaphragm, often caused by the tightening or shortening of the esophagus. This enlarges the small opening of the diaphragm and part of the stomach is pulled up into the chest. The upper part of the esophagus is innervated by the ventral branch of the vagus nerve, and a hiatal hernia often occurs when there is vagal dysfunction.

Most people with this condition usually have difficulty breathing and sometimes have acid reflux or heartburn.

Rosenberg treats hiatal hernias and COPD with basic exercises and a technique that was adapted from visceral osteopathy that lengthens and relaxes the esophagus. This immediately results in the disappearance of breathing difficulties.

Shoulder, Neck and Head Pain

The two major muscles found in the shoulder and neck are the trapezius and sternocleidomastoid. These muscles are innervated by the spinal accessory nerve (CN XI). Any dysfunction in CN XI can result in stiffness and pain felt in the neck and shoulders. Improving the function of the vagal nerve (CN X) and CN XI with exercises can eliminate the pain and ease the tension in these muscles. CN X and CN XI are closely related. They are among the cranial nerves necessary for social engagement.

Migraine Headaches

Although some research studies argue that the fundamental causes of migraines are not yet known, which makes them hard to treat, others have linked the causes of migraines to psychological situations and conditions such as bipolar disorder, anxiety, and activities of the dorsal branch of the vagus nerve. This is quite interesting when viewed from the polyvagal theory perspective. Rosenberg discovered that improvement of the vagal function and also the release of tension in the trapezius and sternocleidomastoid muscles using the pertinent trigger points can help in relieving a migraine in a few minutes.

Bipolar Disorder

Bipolar disorder is a pattern of behavior underlined by seasons of emotional highs alternating with periods of depressive behavior.

Periods of elation and euphoria are followed by periods of low energy and depression. From the viewpoint of the polyvagal theory, the manic/euphoric state is due to the stimulation of the spinal sympathetic chain.

Post-Traumatic Stress Disorder

Ideally, humans possess a resilient autonomic nervous system which often bounces back after a traumatic occurrence. In the case of PTSD, trauma leaves a person not in a state of chronic stress but in a state of dorsal vagal activity which results in depression.

The autonomic system has the capacity to regulate itself. When we feel that our environment is safe, our bodies are relaxed and we are free to socially engage with others.

Anxiety and Panic Attacks

It is normal to get anxious at some point in our lives especially when faced with challenges or in making a major life decision. However, anxiety disorders comprise of more than temporary fear and worry. The anxiety in individuals suffering from an anxiety disorder does not just go away but gets worse over time. This feeling of anxiety can affect and meddle with the daily activities of the individual, thus making them less productive. Fear is a psychological process that can result in immobilization (via the dorsal vagal center) or mobilization (via the sympathetic chain). Fear increases the release of stress hormones which increase heart rate and breathing rate. These symptoms are similar to those of anxiety. In a state of anxiety, worrying thoughts chronically plague the mind.

Panic attacks are short ordeals of terror and uncertainty. They emerge suddenly and might peak within a few minutes, although one can remain uncomfortable for hours. Panic attacks and anxiety are often managed with exercises or hands-on techniques that can bring an individual out of dorsal vagal activation or sympathetic nervous system activation to that of social engagement and communication.

Benefits of the Polyvagal Theory

The benefits of the polyvagal theory cannot be overemphasized. The theory has been very applicable therapeutically, socially and behaviorally. It provides a broadened knowledge of the biological responses to safety and danger; this is based on the delicate connectivity between the gut, body language, facial expressions and voices around us. This is why a soothing voice or a tender face can actively transform our feelings.

It explains why seeing and hearing the voices of the people we love the most brings a feeling of calmness and safety while being disregarded and ignored can accelerate agitation and even mental collapse. In essence, Porges' theory helps us see beyond the fight-or-flight response when understanding trauma. It focuses on social relationships first, aiming to heal them. In medical and psychological research and studies, the polyvagal theory and vagal tone have been very helpful in understanding the physiological basis of several disorders.

The benefits and advantages of the polyvagal theory can be further subdivided into:

1.   Biobehavioral regulation

2.   Social communication

3.   Therapeutic and clinical application

Biobehavioral Regulation

The nervous system is not developed only for survival in dangerous and life-threatening circumstances but also to encourage social communication and bonds in environments that are considered safe.

During the developmental stages of a human particularly in the last trimester and the first year postpartum, the autonomic system changes rapidly. These are necessary changes that give the infant the ability to breathe, access food and maintain body temperature, all basic biological needs. There are also a series of changes in the capability of the infant to modulate physiological and behavioral states through communication with another human such as the mother. The theory suggests that the developmental changes in the neural pathway that oversees the autonomic state procures a neural platform that bolsters the enhancing abilities of the infant to make a connection between people and objects in a constantly changing environment. However, as the neural mechanisms for self-regulation improve under physiological conditions, the dependency and reliance of the infant on others decreases thus, enabling social communication to go beyond searching for basic survival needs such a food, water, clothing and safety and become involved in social engagements.

Clinical Application of the Theory in the Human Fetus

In the human fetus especially under normal conditions, the heart rate is highly variable. This is arbitrated by the vagus nerve. Lengthened withdrawal of vagal influence on the heart results in the physiological vulnerability of the heart to the influence of dorsal vagal control which eventually results in bradycardia (decreased heart rate). It is noteworthy that the onset of the decreased heart rate is often preceded by tachycardia (increased heart rate) which is an indication of the abrupt effect of ventral vagal control withdrawal.

Social Communication/ Social Engagement System

The polyvagal theory is one that connects the evolution of the autonomic nervous system to emotions, facial expressions, affective experience, vocal communication, and social behavior. The theory explains the emergence of a relationship between the nerves controlling the face and heart through evolution. This relationship between the face and the heart is what created the structures necessary for the social engagement system that connects the gestures, facial expression and voiced intonation with bodily feelings. The social engagement system contains a control unit in the cortex of the upper motor neurons that regulates brainstem nuclei (lower motor neurons) which in turn control special visceral efferent pathways to regulate facial muscles, muscles of the middle ear (which differentiate human voices from background noise), muscles of mastication, laryngeal and pharyngeal muscles, and the muscle responsible for turning the head in different directions. The polyvagal theory illustrates how the maturation and modulation of the autonomic nervous system forms a neural base on which social behavior and trust in relationships are built.

The social engagement system is intricately related to stress reactions. The anatomical structures involved in the social engagement system interact neurophysiologically with the hypothalamic-pituitary-adrenal (HPA) axis, neuropeptides found in oxytocin, anti-diuretic hormone (ADH)/vasopressin and the immune system. The social engagement system becomes effective from birth and quickly develops to aid communication and interaction with the environment. Infants communicate with their caregivers by making facial expressions (such as a grimace or a smile) and vocalizations (such as crying and laughing) to engage and attract the attention of their caregivers.

Phylogeny concentrates on the neural systems we have and behaviors we exhibit that have evolved or been modified from those of our genetically related ancestors. Firstly, the three responses suggested by the polyvagal theory (mobilization, immobilization and the ventral vagal complex responsible for emotion, motion, and communication) are the outcomes of unique neurophysiological systems. Secondly, these unique neuropsychological systems are a phylogenetically-dependent hierarchy, such as the use of cranial nerves to modulate and regulate facial expressions and gestures in mammals, the inhibitory vagal system which it shares with primitive vertebrates such as fish and amphibians, and the sympathetic adrenal system it shares with several other vertebrates including reptiles. These stages represent various phylogenetic stages in neural development. Hence, it can be said that the nervous system phylogenetically evolved to support a wider range or spectrum of physiological states and behaviors. These physiological states include those we often associate with stress and positive social behavior. The polyvagal theory is also said to affect stage presence and vocal communication; this includes the visceral effect of the voice on the listener.

Therapeutic and Clinical Benefits of the Polyvagal Theory

The polyvagal theory describes how people respond to danger and life-threatening experiences and how abusive and traumatic occurrences or situations might retune the nervous system in such a way that these individuals react to friends defensively as though they are enemies. This theory is effective in helping therapists and practitioners understand and recognize the characteristics that activate defensive systems in children, teenagers and adults.

Mindfulness-Based Movement

Mindfulness-based movement (MBM) is a modern intervention that promotes a wide spectrum of physical activities and behaviors during and following cancer treatment. It recognizes the significant health benefits that are derived from both decreasing sedentary behavior and improving moderate to rigorous forms of physical activity. MBM is often delivered as a group-mediated intervention that stimulates positive emotions and draws on the cheerful nature of the various forms of movement. The concept of MBM is based on the polyvagal theory. In the view of Porges, playful and energetic forms of physical activity that involve others serve as a neural exercise that facilitates patients in transitioning from aroused motoric states that are associated with physical movements to calm states. From the viewpoint of polyvagal theory, MBM acts as a neural exercise whereby physiological states can be juggled by exercise, focused mindful attention and social engagement.

Autism Spectrum Disorder The polyvagal theory states that individuals on the autism spectrum have a decreased ability to interact socially with other individuals because they have not learned to process complicated social data. Hence, these individuals may continue to interpret and react to the actions of others as threats and might rapidly jump into the fight-flight-freeze response and eventually shut down. This is a result of the high vagal activation experienced by an individual with autism spectrum disorder (ASD), and this has been properly illustrated by the polyvagal theory. The theory explains that during childhood these individuals experienced a diversion of the vagal system toward the safety of the body, thus making this the focus of the developing child. During a bout of immobilization, the body becomes agitated or painful has difficulty digesting food, and experiences an inward shift of focus which reduces interaction with the outside world. The natural integration of the social engagement system does therefore not occur, and this might make the child unable to learn to use their social engagement system thus making it function on autopilot. This disposes the vagus nerve towards immobilization, and the nervous system of the child does not get fully developed. Instead of the primitive and adaptive systems functioning harmoniously, they end up being separate from each other, and the system of the child is in a state of distress. This is to say that the child loses out on what the full integration of the social engagement system has to offer, and their senses are mostly offline. The polyvagal system has its foundation on stress response or response to trauma that occurred previously. This could be a physical alteration of the vagus nerve, a fear that often presents itself at birth or in-utero, or an emotional trauma.

Conclusion

The autonomic nervous system can be regarded as a self-regulatory system. It regulates most of the activities of the visceral organs and it is closely related to the vagus nerve. The polyvagal theory has its basis in the vagus nerve and the autonomic nervous system. The polyvagal theory which was proposed by Dr. Stephen Porges has been a helpful and important tool in understanding the concepts and foundation of various disorders. It has also broadened the understanding of the social engagement and communication system and how it affects individuals and various conditions. The theory links the evolution of the autonomic system and the phylogenetic hierarchy which is divided into three subsystems. This helps us understand the role of the vagus nerve and its effects on the different organs it innervates. This theory also explains how the vagus nerve and the ANS affect daily life. Its therapeutic and clinical applications cannot be overemphasized as it has helped therapists and scientists understand the underlying causes of some disorders and discover better treatment approaches. Stanley Rosenberg is one such therapist who has understood the vagus nerve and its healing power and has used the knowledge acquired from the polyvagal theory to formulate a better therapeutic approach to certain conditions.

Chapter Three: Stephen Porges'

Polyvagal Theory

The term "polyvagal" is derived from the words "polus" and "vagal". "Polus" implies several whereas "vagal" relates to the vagus that is the cranial nerve. The cranial nerve stems directly from the brain stem, relaying data between the brain and the body, primarily from regions of the neck.

The polyvagal theory highlights the autonomic nervous system and claims an association between one's facial features and their physical internal responses like changes in digestion or organ function. The polyvagal theory specializes in the importance of phyletic changes within the neural regulation of the body and phylogenetic shifts providing insight into the accommodative operation of each physiology and behavior of an individual. This theory suggests that social interaction between an individual and their environment could be a neuro-exercise. However, before divulging on it, let us briefly discuss the autonomic system and the way it operates.

The nerve fibers of the autonomic nervous system (ANS) exit at the brain stem or at the spinal cord and converge in a cluster of nerve cells called an autonomic ganglion. They then connect with internal organs. Sensors are present throughout the body that deliver messages to the brain (known as afferent nerve fibers). The main responsibility of the ANS is to manage the operation of the body's internal organs including the heart, gastrointestinal tract, lungs, kidneys, epithelial duct, liver, eyes, adrenal medulla, sweat glands of the skin, and also the salivary and lacrimal glands (responsible for secretion and tears). This same system is the main mechanism in charge of the fight-or-flight response. It can be broken down into 3 branches: the enteric nervous system, the sympathetic nervous system and the parasympathetic nervous system. Amongst these three, the sympathetic and parasympathetic systems are usually mentioned because of their control over the functions of the previously mentioned organs and the way they respond in various situations. The enteric nervous system is the intrinsic nervous system of the digestive tract and is regulates secretions within the gut.

The sympathetic system is responsible for the stimulation of the fight-flight-freeze response and corresponds with arousal and energy generation. The parasympathetic system is responsible for the body's rest, feed, digest and sexual arousal responses.

The polyvagal theory has benefited both professionals and the average person. More than just the insights it gives on exactly how the body works, it also helps us understand why the body is responding in certain ways and what techniques can be used in combating harmful responses. Everything we experience has a link to a potential behavioral pattern, and these patterns have causes and solutions that many are unaware of. The polyvagal theory reveals new insights about how the body works and awaits promising and exciting new physiological discoveries in the future.

About Stephen W. Porges

When it comes to the world of neuroscience, there are few people who have made a positive impact more than Stephen Porges. At Indiana University and the University of Carolina, he is a distinguished scientist. He has been the coordinator of the Brain-Body Center at the university of Chicago.

Among many other positions, he served as the chair of the department of human development and as president of several societies for the biobehavioral sciences. He has also received several awards, one of them being from the Institute of Mental Health Research. He was warmly embraced as a visiting professor at the National Institute of Child Health and Human Development Laboratory of Ethology.

One of his greatest awards or achievements undoubtedly revolves around the patent which he was recently awarded.

This patent would give him the exclusive right to examine the neural regulation of the heart. Despite all his achievements, one of the things of paramount concern is his development of the polyvagal theory.

He would go on to propose this theory in 1994. His aim was to bring to the forefront the various patterns the brain is accustomed to using throughout our lives. To say that this theory has caused a wave of other research would surely be an understatement. Among this research have come about other effective forms of treatment for psychiatric, behavioral and other related disorders of the body and brain.

Porges has written a number of books with his latest on the therapies that make use of the polyvagal theory. The "Safe and Sound Protocol" was first founded by him and it is by this protocol that almost 1500 therapists have found useful employment. Stephen Porges is assuredly a genius in the area of brain and nerve function.

Comprehensive Guide to the Polyvagal Theory

Understanding brain chemistry is like understanding a complex theory or a cyclone. It is not a physical entity, so understanding the dynamics behind it can be difficult. When it comes to the nervous system, Stephen Porges' theory gives counselors an image of the nervous system, which will in turn help us understand it better.

Stephen Porges developed the polyvagal theory out of his experiments and research on the vagus nerve. The vagus nerve is activated by the parasympathetic nervous system, which serves as a calming mechanism for our nervous system.

Dr. Porges goes on to explain that the polyvagal theory helps us understand how our body responds to different situations. These reactions are based on how the autonomic nervous system has grown and evolved or changed throughout the history of its biological process. This change results in the production of several circuits that function in a systematic hierarchy, which enables the newer circuits to inhibit the older ones that serve as a defense mechanism. Viewing it in terms of psychotherapy, it can be concluded that most chronic diseases stem from a malfunctioning of the autonomic nervous system. The polyvagal theory shows us that the way we respond to our environment depends on this biological process pattern where the neurocircuits could represent social interactions.

Before the development of the polyvagal theory, the nervous system was merely viewed as a 2-part system where each one complements the other. The polyvagal theory now reveals a third type of system reaction which Stephen Porges calls the "social engagement system", which is a combination of the activation and calming effects that work without the influence of the vagus nerve. The social engagement system is responsible for our social interactions. This system helps us to be versatile and cope with different situations as they come.

The two main systems of the ANS help us handle dangerous situations. Most counselors only know of the two defense mechanisms, namely fight-or-flight and rest-and-digest (or freeze-or-faint), which are activated by the two divisions of the ANS, the sympathetic nervous system and the parasympathetic nervous system, respectively., The polyvagal theory explains that the branches of the vagus nerve calm the body. For instance, the dorsal branch of the vagus nerve regulates freeze-or-faint responses, and this response can give the person a feeling of fatigue or light-headedness. If the dorsal nerves are shut down, we become immediately immobilized. The dorsal branch affects the lungs, heart and below the diaphragm, and is generally concerned with activities involved in digestion. The ventral branch of the cranial nerves affects the top of the diaphragm and regulates the social engagement system. The ventral cranial nerve allows for activation in a more nuanced manner than that of the sympathetic system.

The ventral cranial nerve fires so quickly that it takes only milliseconds, unlike the sympathetic activation that involves many chemical reactions which take seconds to complete. Furthermore, once chemical fight-or-flight responses have been activated, the body needs about 10–20 minutes to return to its initial state. The ventral cranial nerve does not use chemical reactions of this nature, so it is easier to produce quick changes between panicking and fainting.

The ventral cranial nerve is connected to a special pneumogastric pathway that goes from the brain stem all the way to the gut and is also connected to muscles that are in the face and head. These muscles coordinate listening, facial expressions, vocalization and gestures. This nerve works with the gut to regulate the involuntary state of our body, assuming it is in a state of health, growth, and restoration. When ventral cranial nerve activation fails, behaviors relating to mental states like rage and anxiety ensue. The polyvagal theory calls this the immobilization state.

The polyvagal theory helps us understand the responses our body experiences if it doesn't go into fight-or-flight mode when faced with dangerous situations. These responses are called impulsive reflexes. For instance, if you experience abuse and allow the abuse to continue, it is not voluntary. Our body reactions are based on our awareness, history, and experiences in childhood, adulthood, workplaces, school life, etc. We are conscious of the physical response even though we may not remember what led to that reaction.

In his book "The Polyvagal Theory: Neurophysiological Foundations of Emotions, Attachment, Communication and Self-Regulation", Porges states that the polyvagal theory emphasizes the neuroanatomical and neurophysiological differences between the two branches of the vagus nerve and proposes that every branch of the cranial nerve is linked to a special adaptive behavior and a physiological response to a dangerous event.

The theory further goes on to explain the link between the functioning of our brain and the regulation of the viscera. It explains what happens when the body becomes immobilized (or shuts down) and the response it gives. Before the theory was developed, people traumatized by things like war or abuse were usually labeled as having **Post-Traumatic Stress Disorder (PTSD).** The physiological marker of this disorder was expected to be sympathetic activation or high cortisol levels. But this outdated model did not explain why some patients were emotionless or mentally and emotionally dissociated. It only worked for patients who were under high stress and required some level of calmness in their lives. It did not acknowledge, in any way, the immobilization (shutting down) defense mechanism.

As seen earlier, mammals evolved and this evolution led to immobilization since there was a continuous threat to life.

Immobilization results in a low pulse rate, and sometimes the heart shuts down completely. The cranial nerve is a component of the lower region of the diaphragm that regulates target organs if the sympathetic and parasympathetic systems are dormant in an exceptionally safe situation. But in a dangerous situation, the cranial nerve moves quickly, and since it regulates biological processes, it causes urination, defecation, and sometimes fainting. For victims of trauma, the cranial nerve becomes dysfunctional, which can lead to a bout of constipation followed by diarrhea.

What the polyvagal theory states is that we have two primary defense pathways with an additional third defense pathway signaled by the vagus nerve that acts below the diaphragm but still has a significant impact on the heart.

Social Interactions and Polyvagal Theory

When it comes to the autonomic nervous system, it can be aptly divided into at least three classes of development. These levels of development are often described as phylogenetic stages. These stages are often connected with the three unique classes of systems namely immobilization, mobilization, and social engagement.

In his research, Stephen Porges used the term "social engagement" for several reasons. One of them would be the effects the ventral nerve has had on some parts of the ear (middle ear). The role of the middle ear is to ensure background noise is filtered out and does not affect our concentration when trying to focus on something. The ventral nerve also helps control facial expressions, the mouth and vocalization, ensuring the right sounds for the right occasion.

An example of social engagement would be what happens when we encounter a dog. Dogs have many social behaviors, one of which is the tendency to either fight you or take to your heels if they feel threatened. While this may be true of certain dogs, others may want to play and engage with the human. This usually happens when the dog senses that the human is safe and friendly.

Similarly, people usually display a playful attitude and feel they can be themselves upon sensing they are somewhere safe. People tend to come out of their shells and become socially engaged at this point. However, if the environment seems to be toxic or unsafe, it is not unusual to see someone become defensive in order to protect themselves from the harm which they sense is coming.

The vagus nerve plays a large role in our body. When we feel rejected, we tend to have what is often described as a visceral response. In other words, the vagal nerve would often deactivate. This leads to one of two scenarios: either we experience an immobilizing or dissociating response, or we experience the sympathetic response. The reason for this can be traced back to the cranial nerve. The cranial nerve is often at rest, and this ensures that we fully experience the sensations highlighted in the example above when necessary.

Once in the fight-or-flight state, everything we see or do will be altered. Faces that are naturally neutral would seem harsh or even aggressive to us and put us in defense mode. If we feel trapped, we have the tendency to shut down, or mentally and emotionally dissociate, and try to understand the situation that we find ourselves in.

Understanding the polyvagal theory and how our nervous system works would ensure that we have a better understanding of social engagement and the other mechanisms we have discussed. We would also have a better understanding of our inclinations based on our past experiences and traumas. Understanding the polyvagal theory is essential to improving our lives and understanding of ourselves both now and in the future.

Benefits of the Polyvagal Theory

There are many benefits of the polyvagal theory and the way it identifies the third response system. This has been one of the most essential discoveries in neurobiology this century. It expresses the utmost connection between the vagal nerve and certain psychological dysfunctions.

The polyvagal theory gives a basic illustration of how vagus nerve activation or dysfunction is expressed in terms of signs and symptoms of conditions such as depression, autism, anxiety as well as other psychopathological issues present.

Consistent with what the theory expands on, this symptom cluster is found to originate from the vagal system. The polyvagal theory helps us to be able to translate compromised or unusual social behavior in humans from another perspective. The theory proposes that social behavior is limited by mental state. This speculation goes on to emphasize that mobilization and immobilization behaviors are found to be adaptive strategies in a challenging situation.

Undoubtedly, a state of calmness yields more positive social behaviors in humans, as calmness stimulates the activities of the brain that form the social engagement system. Due to this, we will carefully focus on the ways spontaneous, positive social activities affect mental state in comparison to conventional medication as a form of intervention.

One of the treatment methods outlined in the polyvagal theory is a behavioral intervention that makes use of acoustic stimulation to initiate or support social behavior; it was tested on youngsters diagnosed with autism. The Listening Project is an intervention based on this research and is backed up by many principles derived from the polyvagal theory.

It is important to understand how the brain stem works. It controls the muscles of the head, such as those of the face, mouth, mid-ear, the pharynx and the larynx. These muscles work together in a connection known as the integrated social engagement system, and this controls actions like vocalization, hearing, sight, and different facial expressions, or the art of expressivity.

When there is a dysfunction with the regulation of the muscles in the face, issues can occur such as inappropriate facial expression, eyelid sagging or drooping, apparent difficulties in paying attention, and much more. Such facial expressions and behaviors can have different patterns and symptoms which are common to various psychopathologies such as depression, anxiety, PTSD, autism, etc. Dysfunction in facial muscle control can also influence our emotional states in times of anger, grief, loneliness, rage and more.

Next are the middle ear muscles. These play a vital role in recognizing and extracting the human voice from other sounds in the environment. Sounds reach the middle ear muscles, but for lower frequency sounds, the middle ear structure filters them out in an acoustic environment, making them harder to hear. This is why problems in hearing human voices can occur even for people who have more normal hearing.

Next is the neural operation of the middle ear muscles. These are responsible for managing the facial muscles involved in looking and listening as well as intonation of the voice when speaking.

The part of the brain containing the lower motor neurons that manage social engagement, such as facial expressions and intonation, is located in the lower part of the brain stem. These lower motor neurons are later regulated by the upper motor neurons found in the motor cortex of the brain. When fight-or-flight or immobilization responses are activated, there is the idea of cortical controlling of these lower neurons.

Primal systems such as those controlled by the lower motor neurons of the brain stem are dependent on the entirety of the neural structures. These have evolved to ensure survival through the resources that control mobility, be it fighting or fleeing, or through immobilization which includes freezing and death feigning or fainting.

The Listening Project intervention takes into consideration that a person with smaller muscles may feel drained quicker. This intervention showed that most of the participants felt fatigued after about an hour of listening. They also slept better at night due to the relative feedback from their systems and the exhaustion from listening, almost feeling like they had run a few miles.

The benefits surrounding the polyvagal theory are more than meets the eye. When practiced well, it offers hope and help to people all over the world. It gives detailed insight into how the body works, and this book helps show how one can put these into practice with certain conditions that are affected by the vagus nerve and could be causing deterioration throughout the body.

As mentioned, this polyvagal theory was developed from Porges' different experiments with the vagus nerve which proved positive. It is also known that the vagus nerve acts parasympathetically, helping to calm various responses and mechanics in the body. It helps in balancing sympathetically activated areas but in a much more advanced way than was previously understood. Understandably, vagal dysfunction has also been linked to many health concerns including anxiety and depression, which may not have been considered in the past.

Facing unresolved trauma from the past can trigger the fight-or-flight state, often resulting in anxiety. The polyvagal theory shows how we can channel this anxiety into various positive activities such as singing, dancing and cleaning to help us calm down.

However, some trauma victims find it hard to healthily channel this fight-or-flight related anxiety, which is why their bodies tend to shut down. Practical ways of handling this appear in later chapters.

Conclusion

The major problem encountered when treating trauma is when it is filed as a general category of disorders related to stress, and this categorization has led to neglecting how the body generally responds when dealing with life-threatening situations. Most people assume that we have only one defense mechanism which is the fight-or-flight response. This response is what is primarily referred to in books when discussing reactions to stress or anxiety, when what should really also be discussed is the way the body immobilizes in reaction to life threats.

Immobilization is a unique physiological state that is dangerous for mammals. This can be observed in house rats when caught in a trap or within the jaws of a cat; at first sight, we see and presume that the rat is dead, but upon closer observation, it turns out to be feigning death. However, this response is not conscious. We learn that it is an adaptive biological reaction to the inability to access or use the fight-or-flight mechanism to defend or escape. This was not previously understood.

The polyvagal theory helps us understand that the nervous system has a second defense system and that the choice between fight-or-flight and immobilization/shutdown is an unconscious one, an involuntary decision. It proposes that outside our own awareness, the nervous system is constantly alert, evaluating environmental risks and prioritizing behaviors that are adaptive and unconscious. We also discover that the response may vary between individuals, that is, while some situations may trigger fight-or-flight in some, it may trigger immobilization/shutdown for others. This is why a person's response is to be considered more carefully than the event itself.

Enjoying this book?

Please leave a review because we would love to hear your feedback, opinions and advice to create better products and services for you! Thank you for your support. You are greatly appreciated!"

Chapter Four: Stanley Rosenberg's

Polyvagal Theory

In previous chapters, we have broken down the concepts of the polyvagal theory, and we have reviewed Stephen Porges' work surrounding this theory. The other important contribution to this area of study is the Stanley Rosenberg polyvagal theory which is gaining traction and becoming very relevant in this field.

Great people like Jean-Pierre Barral, Benjamin Shield, and Alain Gehin, leaders in the manual therapies field with whom Stanley Rosenberg has worked with throughout the years, have commented on the great work of this scientist. The major purpose of Rosenberg's work is to help people understand the importance of the cranial nerves and how they serve as keys to improving our overall well-being. It is important to note that his theory builds on the existing Stephen Porges theory. The Stanley Rosenberg polyvagal theory draws extensively on how the cranial and vagal nerves help us to determine our emotional, psychological, and physical state.

In this chapter, we will review the full breakdown of the Stanley Rosenberg polyvagal theory and how it contributes to the autonomic nervous system. This theory, written and postulated by Stanley Rosenberg, is a practical guide meant to help access the healing power embedded in the vagal nerve.

About Stanley Rosenberg

The creator of this polyvagal theory is none other than Stanley Rosenberg who is a therapist and an American-born author. He has been a practicing Rolfer since 1983. In 1987, he began practicing craniosacral therapy and has become one of the most successful therapists in the country. As a young scientist, he trained under the great scientist Alain Gehin who is currently a doctor of manipulative medicine. The people he has worked with include: Giorgia Milne who is certified in Biodynamic Cranial Touch/Stillness Touch, Jean-Pierre Barral, an osteopath and developer of the visceral manipulation technique, and Benjamin Shield, a PhD and Rolfer.

Stanley Rosenberg is a well-trained and seasoned Rolfer based in Denmark, having much experience to learn on. Over the year, he has taught craniosacral therapy and Rolfing to individuals and corporate bodies around the world. He is the first craniosacral therapist who successfully applied craniosacral therapy together with other therapeutic techniques.

Stanley Rosenberg was once the director of a school in Denmark where he taught scar tissue release, visceral massage, bio tensegrity and structural integration. While in Denmark, he published four books which include *Hwa Yu Tai Chi*, *Nevermore Pain in the Back*, *Pain Relief with Osteomassage*, and *Nevermore Stiff Neck*.

His book *Accessing the Healing Power of the Vagus Nerve* has received significant positive acclaim by several bodies in the medical field around the world. The foreword of the book was written by the originator of the polyvagal theory himself, Stephen Porges. In his foreword, he acknowledged the writer of the book and urged all the readers of this great manuscript to pay close attention to the instructions and teachings laid out in the pages of the book. Stanley Rosenberg wrote extensively on the healing power of the vagal nerve, how individuals can understand its power, and how we can utilize this understanding to help us heal ourselves.

Science and medicine are the fields that Stanley Rosenberg has shown prime expertise in. Many of his courses can be found and accessed on his personal website. Stanley Rosenberg is seen as a leader in his field, and his works attest to this. His findings on the polyvagal theory and the craniosacral therapy have changed the entire concept behind the theory and, over the years, he has become one of the most sought-after therapists. To fully understand these concepts, I strongly recommend reading his book, *Accessing the Healing Power of the Vagus Nerve.*

Guide on the Stanley Rosenberg Theory

The entire concept behind the creation of this theory will leave you speechless. In this theory, Stanley Rosenberg explains in full detail how the vagus nerve in the human body helps us determine how to react to everything concerning our emotional and psychological state.

Before we go deeper into this guide, we will give you a very concrete introduction and explanation of the vagus nerve, since it forms the basis of all that Stanley Rosenberg's theory is about.

The vagus nerve plays a strong role in enabling us to react appropriately with other people. It is the longest nerve in the autonomic nervous system (which will be explained in later sections) and it is most often described as the tenth cranial nerve in this system. When it comes to physical and emotional stress, this nerve also plays a large part.

The vagus nerve sends out sensory fibers into the visceral organs from the brainstem. When it comes to fight-or-flight responses, the vagus nerve also takes full responsibility by flooding the body with the stress hormones cortisol and adrenaline.

When the vagus nerve lacks sufficient stimulation, it may

lead to fainting. Vagal syncope is always a response to stress. During vagal syncope, loss of consciousness can occur because blood flow is being redirected to your brain.

All these outlined points show the great significance of the vagus nerve in the body. One of the most significance points is how the vagus nerve helps us to heal properly. This is the core concept behind the work that Stanley Rosenberg developed from the work of Stephen Porges.

The autonomic nervous system, as explained in a previous chapter, is described as a division of the peripheral nervous system that connects muscles and glands to the internal organs of the human body. In medical terms, it is described as a control system that helps to control all bodily functions.

The PNS is in charge of everything outside the central nervous system, which includes the nerves. The main work of the PNS is to link different body parts to the CNS. It also enables the brain and spinal cord to interact with other areas of the body by sending and receiving information. It is through this process that we can react to different environmental stimuli.

For you as the reader to properly understand the concept behind the Stanley Rosenberg polyvagal theory, proper understanding of how the autonomic nervous system works is required. The study of the ANS and the vagus nerve are what make up what we know as the polyvagal theory. If at this point in the book, you still find it difficult to understand the concept behind the ANS, I strongly suggest you go back to the beginning of the book and read it again. The essence of the polyvagal theory is to help identify what goes on when you have visceral experiences or visceral feelings and how they relate to the vagus nerve. The whole concept of the polyvagal theory created originally by Stephen Porges was for the study of social, emotional and stress-induced behavior in humans. The Stanley Rosenberg polyvagal theory is more of a spin-off from the original theory written by Porges. In this theory, Stanley Rosenberg states that the vagus nerve has healing power and more than we know or imagine. In his book, *Accessing the Healing Power of the Vagus Nerve*, Stanley Rosenberg writes extensively on how powerful the vagus nerve is. The vagus nerve, as explained by Stanley Rosenberg, helps calm the body and introduces the body to the welcome touch. Rosenberg stresses that there are several exercises someone suffering from several forms of mental, emotional and psychological stress can do. In the medical field today, these exercises and self-help strategies are very relevant, and they have helped many patients, especially those with complex cases.

The more these exercises are performed, the more visible

changes in the body are noticeable. These changes are always a result of the increase in vagal tone. When referring to responses of the vagal nerve, we must not fail to mention vagal tone.

You might ask, *What is vagal tone?* Vagal tone simply refers to the activities of the vagal nerve. These activities result in various effects including vasodilation of vessels and overall glandular activity in the body. Vagal tone is in charge of accessing all the processes that are altered by a change in the parasympathetic function of the body.

You might be asking, *Can vagal tone in the human body be measured?* The simple answer is, yes. Vagal tone of the body can be measured either invasively or non-invasively. The non-invasive procedure simply involves investigation of heart rate. The invasive procedure involves constant stimulation of the vagal nerve by either electrical or manual techniques.

So what is the importance of vagal tone to this whole concept of the Stanley Rosenberg polyvagal theory? Let's break it down.

The vagus nerve is like the regulator in the body, and the tone of the vagus nerve regulates how active it is. Low vagal tone does not stimulate the vagus nerve while high vagal tone does. When vagal tone is high, applying the self-help exercises to access its healing power is much easier. As soon as you begin to experience stress, the most important thing you can do is to try out various exercises to help you improve your vagal tone. This will help you calm down and heal faster. The exercises you need are all listed in the benefits section below. While reading through the self-help exercises recommended by Stanley Rosenberg, be sure to try them out.

Vagal tone is very important and in the later sections of this chapter, we will discuss how important vagal tone is while reviewing the benefits of the Stanley Rosenberg polyvagal theory.

In the Stanley Rosenberg theory, vagus nerve stimulation increases vagal tone in the body. By working with the vagus nerve, healing processes may be initiated. In the medical field, stimulation of the vagal nerve is mostly used as an additional treatment for depression and epilepsy. When it comes to the stimulation of the vagal nerve, Stanley Rosenberg's theory becomes very relevant. In the study of the application of craniosacral therapy, in his work with John Upledger, Rosenberg was able to combine the concepts of craniosacral therapy with the polyvagal theory to create a new healing paradigm. Craniosacral therapy is also another well-received therapy in the medical field. It is described as a form of alternative therapy that makes use of gentle touch to examine the inert part of the synarthrodial joints of the cranium. In the study of craniosacral therapy, most researchers have claimed that it is very harmful and can cause many side effects, especially for infants. This is why most physicians recommend using the Stanley Rosenberg polyvagal theory. As stated previously, it is a combination of the polyvagal theory and the studies that exist on craniosacral therapy.

That concludes the overview of the Stanley Rosenberg theory. In the next section of this chapter, we will discuss how beneficial Rosenberg's theory is and how individuals and clients can properly utilize this theory for overall physical and mental health.

Benefits of the Stanley Rosenberg Theory

The Stanley Rosenberg Theory has been shown to have many benefits, especially on the human body in the long-term. Stimulating the vagal nerve allows us to access great healing powers for self-help. People all over the world have used this theory and gained tremendous results in recent years. Many of these people have come forward and given justification for why they prefer this theory and how they were able to use it in regaining control of their bodies, returning them back to their previous states.

In this section, we will outline 6 great benefits of Stanley Rosenberg's theory and how this theory is beneficial to the overall wellness and development of the body.

1.   Its self-help strategies help patients to find their innate healing potential faster.

When Rosenberg postulated this theory, he wrote about several exercises that could be used to restore all the social properties embedded in the vagal system. Many have stated that by doing these self-help exercises, they begin to feel relieved. This is because, with these specific exercises, the autonomic nervous system gradually returns to a state of emotional and physical safety from a state of stress and depression.

2.   It helps make your brain more active.

Since the autonomic nervous system is mostly situated in the brain, the use of the vagus nerve to access healing powers makes the brain more alive. The brain makes the whole body function, and when you are feeling stressed and depressed, it is your brain and all its activities that suffer. These exercises are helpful because they help your brain develop in such a way that it slowly and gradually becomes sharper. Many have given great testimonies about these exercises and strategies and how they have improved their mental capacities.

3.   Apart from improving brain function and accessing its healing power, physical improvements occur.

The exercises outlined here and in Rosenberg's book help

you not only deal with anxiety, depression and trauma but also to improve physically. Rosenberg has worked with many therapists to teach them how to help their patients administer the self-help techniques outlined in his famous book. While practicing these simple exercises yourself, you will begin to see relevant changes throughout your body, your sleep and sleep habits will improve, and you will speedily recover from trauma.

4.   It is one of the best self-help strategies.

In Rosenberg's book, *Accessing the Healing Power of the Vagus Nerve*, Stephen Porges in the foreword commends Rosenberg's efforts and acclaims that the studies and findings in the book are very important especially in this field. He acknowledged that the combination of the polyvagal theory and the studies of the craniosacral system is a great innovation. Rosenberg's polyvagal theory involves many manipulations to promote a sense of safety and help the body restore itself.

In the medical field, this theory currently stands as one of the best in terms of complete physical and mental restoration.

5.   Once the power of the vagus nerve can be accessed, it helps reduce inflammation.

In simple terms, inflammation is described as a physical

condition where a certain part of the body begins to experience swelling and becomes hot and painful. If not properly treated, it could result in long-term tissue damage. Inflammation is meant to help heal the body after an injury, however, if it persists, it may lead to damage in the organs and blood vessels. The vagus nerve helps to reduce inflammation by resetting the immune system, which reduces production of the proteins that cause inflammation. The lower the vagal tone, the higher the risk of inflammation in the body. This is why knowing how to make use of vagus nerve stimulation is essential for health.

6.   When vagal tone is high, it increases happiness.

This point right here is one of the most emphasized points in the medical and science field. When vagal tone is high, it always leads to feelings of happiness and joy. This is the great work of the vagus nerve and the polyvagal theory.

How To Maintain High Vagal Tone

What are the best ways to keep vagal tone high at all times? The best solutions are as follows:

•   Always breathe slowly and breathe from the diaphragm.

This method always helps to alter heart rate variability. The simplest way to do this is by applying the Rebalance Sequence. The Rebalance Sequence is a 10-minute sequence that helps to increase heart rate variability. Once you slow your breathing down, focus on the direction of the movement of the diaphragm; in doing this, you will change the way your brain stem sends signals to the diaphragm to contract. This is called the 3-D breathing technique.

The following steps are very important when it comes to stimulating vagal tone. By doing these, you will be assured of the best results.

•   Maintain a healthy gut. The gut is closely connected to the enteric nervous system. This system connects the gut to the brain through the vagus nerve. To maintain a healthy gut, always ensure that you are eating the right food. Probiotics help keep the gut healthy and stable. Try to reduce your calorie intake; by doing this, your vagal tone will become more stable.

•   Always wash your face and bathe with cold water. The importance of this cannot be overemphasized. This may come as a difficult task for most, but it is very helpful. Bathing and washing your face with cold water is an ancient Chinese tradition that helps to stimulate the vagus nerve. An alternative to this is what is known as the cold plunge where you sit in hot water and put your face in ice water for 20 seconds. This is highly effective in vagal stimulation.

- Practice meditation.

Meditation helps restore vagal tone and has healing effects on the body. Regular meditation is bound to keep your mind open and allow you to process things faster. Once you apply daily meditation to your routine, the healing processes you need will become easier.

- Reduce the tension in your jaw. When the jaw is not properly aligned, it can lead to low vagal tone. The best thing to do for jaw tension is to stimulate the tissue behind the ear. This is where the vagus nerve branches out. It helps to reduce tissue compression in that area. Once you release the tissues in this area, the connection of the vagus nerve here will improve and function better.

These habits above and others from Rosenberg's book are habits that must be practiced regularly; they are part of the exercises recommended for you to unlock and access the great power of the vagus nerve. You may be wondering at this point, *Why do I have to do all these?* The answer is that all these actions help to stimulate your vagus nerve which helps you to relax.

The Stanley Rosenberg theory combined with the polyvagal theory is the key to well-being. Have you ever imagined how our lives would have been if we did not have the vagal nerve or autonomic nervous system to help whenever we need it? Thanks to Dr. Stephen Porges and Stanley

Rosenberg, we now know how important they are. The mind-body connection in humans would not be possible without the vagus nerve, and thanks to extensive studies done by Rosenberg, we now see its great possibility. Many describe it as a secret, sweet instrument playing inside their head which lowers their physical intensity and helps them calm down. Without all these studies on craniosacral therapy and the polyvagal theory, we may not have discovered this.

By accessing the power of the vagus nerve, you will be able to keep your heart rate in check. Did you know that the vagus nerve is a major contributor to all the activities of the heart? The vagus nerve sends a message to the brain to inform the brain of how we are breathing. The brain then sends a response to the heart.

This is the sole reason why anytime you perform any strenuous activity, your heart begins to beat faster and your breathing increases. Once you are breathing slowly again, your heart rate drops because the vagus nerve sends a message to the brain and the rate of oxygen demand on the myocardium (the heart muscle) is suddenly reduced. The vagus nerve and the ANS are some of the most powerful systems in the body and this theory by Stanley Rosenberg helps us to fully understand and utilize it.

This theory helps us to understand the parasympathetic functions of the body. The vagus nerve plays an important role in the PSNS. As explained in the previous chapter and in chapter one, the PSNS is also known as the rest-and-digest system.

Conclusion

We have reviewed the concepts behind the polyvagal theory and the autonomic nervous system. The previous chapter dwelt extensively on the Stephen Porges polyvagal theory and its benefits to humans and to the medical field in general. In this chapter, we also looked extensively at the Stanley Rosenberg polyvagal theory and how it is closely connected to the original theory of Stephen Porges. We dove a little deeper into the biography of Rosenberg as a therapist and looked at some of his works from around America and Europe.

The Stanley Rosenberg polyvagal theory is an important theory that you must understand, even if you are not in the medical or science field, because it gives us vital information about the physical structure and functions of the body, especially about the vagus nerve and the ANS. This theory, in conjunction with the Stephen Porges theory, helps us to properly access and utilize the power of the vagus nerve for our healing. Whenever we are stressed, depressed, traumatized, anxious or sad, regular practice of these specific exercises and activities can stimulate the vagus nerve which can help you feel relaxed.

The next chapter in this book is a practical guide to applying the polyvagal theory. It simply explains how practitioners and patients can work together to fully apply and utilize the polyvagal theory.

Chapter Five: Practical Guide to Applying the Polyvagal Theory

Introduction

Stanley Rosenberg focuses on the basic intricacies of our lives as individuals and as a society in general. It is not because life is changing more than it has in the past, but the world seems to be going into a stranger form of existence whereas we try to fix one problem and it can lead to a number of unintended outcomes. This makes more grounded people live in anxiety, especially those who are trying to overcome an overwhelming trauma.

People who work with others going through trauma might need to proceed more slowly, as it is understood that the trauma in a person's body partly exists because the body has refused to let it go.

Stephen Porges developed the polyvagal theory which looks at the nervous system and exactly how it responds to stress and danger. It is often described as a 3-part hierarchical system, and as the theory describes, the body assesses stress or danger through certain signals from the environment. Basically, if we begin to perceive stress, sooner or later sympathetic activation comes into play.

The way the brain is wired has not changed much over time. It is designed to protect us from danger of various forms either by fight or by flight, by activation or by deactivation. When we encounter danger, the social engagement system is stimulated first; if we find that it that doesn't do the trick, our activation system engages. That means we are ready to jump into action and our heart rate starts increasing. If the threat gets too large to be managed, the body activates the dorsal vagus system as a last resort. This theory can be applied in various situations as described in the following section.

Anxiety

Anxiety is the body's natural response to stress, and many people experience anxiety from time to time but that doesn't necessarily mean they have an anxiety disorder. This is because anxiety is basically the feeling of apprehension or even fear of future events. People can become anxious in different places and for different reasons. It could occur because of a job interview or a speech or even the first day of school either as a student or as a teacher. These make the brain and the mind more fearful and nervous.

It is well known that anxiety and panic attacks have an

impact on blood pressure and that the vagus nerve connects to various organs in the body. When an organ is not stimulated by the vagus nerve, it can lead to issues ranging from anxiety to stomach-related problems.

Less stimulated or unstimulated vagus nerve branches could be a leading cause of anxiety and panic attacks.

Let's use this example: if your anxiety's root cause is a stomach issue, then when your vagus nerve is stimulated, your vagal tone increases, helping your stomach and solving your anxiety issue. Now you might be wondering exactly how to increase your vagal tone. There are many activities known to increase vagal tone and activation, and they range from breathing exercises to singing, etc. Although these are fantastic methods for stimulation of the vagus nerve, the best method is through the use of cold therapy/ice.

This is a very practical way of relieving yourself of anxiety using the polyvagal theory. When you expose your vagus nerve to cold conditions, it tends to shut down the body's fight-or-flight response to feelings such as anxiety and panic attacks. For example, placing an ice pack at the back of the neck is sure to boost your parasympathetic nervous system. This calms a person down almost immediately as it reduces the heart rate.

Ice packs aren't the only thing that can be used, as even a

cold shower or using ice-cold water on your face accompanied by deep breaths can calm your anxiety.

So next time you feel your anxiety rising or feel a panic attack coming on, go to the freezer and get an ice pack and place it gently at the back of your neck, and don't forget to take deep breaths. In doing so, you'll be able to sense your body calming down.

Depression

The polyvagal theory can be applied to depression in different ways. To understand it better, we have to look at the visceral level of vagal nerve activation through this theory. Mental disorders such as depression are mostly caused by the malfunctioning of the autonomic/vegetative nervous system. Both the parasympathetic and sympathetic systems are dominant while vagal tone is low. In depression, there is a constant level of stress which makes a person consistently feel uneasy and prevents them from behaving appropriately.

This is a reason people suffering from depression lack the passion and drive for many things and are unable to relax. Their sleep is unrefreshing, and they tend to wake up tired. In depression, the "smart vagus" (ventral vagus) system cannot cope with the sympathetic branch of the nervous system.

Naturally, after a stressful experience, the "smart vagus" should be able to enforce a "vagal brake" (vagal stimulation) or sympathetic deactivation, decreasing the heart rate and stabilizing the breathing pattern. However, this action can be blocked by traumatic experiences and this leads to imbalance. So instead of smart vagus activation, the parasympathetic replaces the sympathetic, and this can lead to apathy in a person.

Breathing exercises are a great way to heal depression for various reasons. The key functions of the autonomic nervous system include regulating heart rhythm as well as breathing. These are both controlled by the vagus nerve. Breathing is relaxed and calm when the smart (ventral) vagus is active, while the sympathetic system handles breathing when under stress by causing shorter and shallower breaths.

When you learn to improve your breathing, you can access the vagal brakes (vagal activation causing sympathetic deactivation). People battling depression would need to change several aspects of their breathing including taking deeper breaths in order to expand their lung capacity and to increase oxygen metabolism. There are additional benefits to taking deeper breaths such as building one's self-esteem, confidence, and trust in themselves.

Also note the quality of the exhale because it also affects the sympathetic system. A relaxed breath doesn't just fill your lungs with oxygen, but it comes with acceptance and trust. Breathing therapy is a good way to let go of all obstacles in order to focus on achieving relaxed breathing. By doing so, you are letting go of the trauma that causes the failure of the vagal brake. Breathing exercises can help in restoring the balance by accessing and healing the vagal brake.

Although this could seem like a stressful way of handling depression, progress is made with each relaxed, deep breath which helps you on your path to recovery in everyday life.

Trauma

People who have unresolved trauma or PTSD from an event in the past may pass through life in a version of constant fight-or-flight. The main challenge with this is that it disrupts your everyday life and affects your daily activities. There are, however, ways to channel this fight-or-flight response into other activities that can be soothing and relaxing.

Activities such as cleaning the house, working out in the gym, going on a run, or gardening, for example, are great channels, but they might feel different if done with the intention of engaging the social engagement system. However, this can be difficult for some trauma victims as their fight-or-flight sensations cannot be channeled effectively. This causes the body to shut down and make them feel trapped.

Peter Levine, a colleague and friend of Porges who has studied the basic shutdown responses by observing animals as well as his clients' bodies while walking, explains that coming back from a shutdown requires a person to shudder or shake themselves in order to release the appropriate energy for a fight-or-flight response. This means we can jolt ourselves out of a freeze/shutdown in life-threatening situations. What needs to be done is to help the body move into social engagement activation.

If you feel depressed, shutdown and dissociative because of trauma, getting in touch with your fight-or-flight response could prove positive. A good way is through body awareness techniques which are a part of cognitive behavioral therapy (CBT) and dialectical behavior therapy (DBT). These therapies can help clients slowly move away from their shutdown or dissociative responses and become more engaged.

Shutdown responses can be eradicated by understanding your body and becoming more present while being able to attend to momentary muscular tension. Mind and body therapies help in a wide range of areas in health and well-being.

These therapies can help reactivate a person out of shutdown and can encourage the shifting to fight-or-flight responses. Both the CBT and DBT help teach individuals to assess their safety better. There is a possible link to feeling safe enough and moving into social engagement activation.

Some of the physical symptoms of trauma include tightness in the chest, exhaustion, and a sinking feeling in the stomach, among others. Massage, tai chi, acupuncture, and counseling, for example, are great mind and body therapies that make us feel more in control and calm.

Autism

The polyvagal theory offers a good explanation for most common autistic features such as social difficulties, sensory sensitivity and gut dysfunction, while at the same time proposing strategies to ease the severity of certain features.

Due to the evolution of mammals, parts of the autonomic nervous system came to be integrated with neural pathways that have control over the face and the head. This makes the ANS a great asset to the control and regulation of senses other than the two common ones. This new circuit is very relevant to the polyvagal view on autism as it can inform more primitive circuits and has also evolved to enable prosocial behaviors.

The vagal pathway also involves a new system that originates in part of the brain stem, and this helps in controlling muscles of the face and head and also handles facial expressions, speaking, listening and ingestion. It allows for vocalization and facial expressions which are powerful approaches to engage in different social behaviors.

When this system is shut down, it results in many of the traits present in autism such as poor vocal intonation, lack of facial expressions, hypersensitivity to sound, gut problems, defensive stares, and selective eating, amongst others.

Just as humans are social animals and look at trusted people for safety cues, it may be more difficult for autistic people who neither recognize nor respond to these cues. This is why their bodies detect danger in social engagements.

Transcutaneous vagus nerve stimulation is one way of working with autism. This is a technique whereby an electrical current is applied to the vagus nerve. This nerve runs between the brain and different areas of the body like the heart, the skin and the gastrointestinal tract. As previously mentioned, the vagus nerve is very important to both the physical and emotional responses in the body and enters either fight-or-flight mode, or rest-and-digest.

The vagus nerve can be stimulated electrically through an implanted device or an external device applied to the skin.

If you think this sounds dangerous, you should know that vagus nerve stimulation is an FDA-approved treatment for seizures, and research has shown that this same treatment can be used for depression.

Different research studies have shown that when treated with thoracic vagus nerve stimulation (TVN), children with autism have shown improvement in their behaviors, cognitive functions and of course, seizure frequency.

How to Optimize Your Autonomic Functioning Using the Polyvagal Theory

During the last trimester in utero and the following year after birth, the autonomic nervous system undergoes rapid changes. These changes are necessary so infants can breathe, maintain body temperature, obtain food and much more. Such development is the basic progression in the biology of infants in order to regulate their physiological and behavioral state when interaction with another person takes place, which is most likely the mother at first.

It is thought that these developmental changes and their neural pathways which regulate the autonomic state can provide a neural platform in supporting the abilities of infants to be expanded when they engage with objects as well as people in a frequently changing environment. This causes the emerging behavioral patterns and social interactive needs and desires of a growing infant to be viewed within the context of maturational alterations in their autonomic nervous system.

Since the autonomic nervous system plays a crucial role in a child's survival when they transition from the prenatal to the postnatal environment, it is quite astonishing that the central mechanisms of the autonomic nervous system have been digressive to pediatric medicine.

The nervous system of mammals did not just develop for the sole purpose of surviving in life-threatening and dangerous situations but also to promote social interactions and bonding. In order to achieve this adaptive flexibility, a new neural strategy seeking safer environments has developed while the more primitive neural circuits regulating defensive approaches have been retained. To be able to accommodate both fight-or-flight as well as social engagement behaviors, the modern vagal system in mammals has evolved to enable rapid, adaptive shifts in more autonomic situations.

Three Organizing Principles

There are 3 organizing principles when it comes to the polyvagal theory, namely hierarchy, neuroception and co-regulation.

Hierarchy

The autonomic nervous system responds to sensations in the body and signals from the environment with one of 3 different response. These pathways are activated in a particular order, the order of evolution, when it comes to responding to challenges in a predictable manner. They include the dorsal vagal branch which has to do with immobilization, the sympathetic nervous system for mobilization, and lastly the ventral vagus branch which is in charge of social engagement and connection.

Neuroception

This is a word coined by Dr. Porges himself which he used in describing the various ways the autonomic nervous system responds to people or situations that appear safe, dangerous or life-threatening situations.

Co-regulation

Co-regulation describes how an individual's responses are influenced by the responses of another person. The polyvagal theory identifies co-regulation as an important biological response as it is viewed as necessary in order to sustain life. Through this reciprocal regulation of various autonomic states, we decide whether we feel safe enough to want a connection and create and sustain certain relationships. The autonomic nervous system is thought of as a foundation upon which all life experiences are built. It is viewed as the platform upon which we base all our experiences. The various movements we make in the world such as connecting and isolating, coming and going, etc. are all directed by the ANS.

With supportive, co-regulating relationships, we tend to become much more resilient. These relationships help us master the art of survival, and that is why the ANS is continually learning habits of creating connection and protection in relationships.

It is hopeful to say that early intervention can help in shaping the nervous system as can ongoing experiences. As we know, the brain continuously adapts our responses to different environments and experiences. The ANS is very engaged and we too can influence it as we please. Our nervous system is built to reach out for co-regulation as we experience moments of either safety or danger. The signals conveyed, either of safety or of danger, which are sent from one autonomic nervous system to another can regulate or increase certain reactions.

Optimizing Autonomic Function

Optimizing your autonomic functioning can be done through taking deep breaths, box breathing, cold/ice and gut health.

Deep Breathing

Although this might seem cliché, there is a connection between respiration and heart rate which affects the vagus nerve. This is a good reason why yoga can help reduce overall stress. Breathing exercises can increase vagal tone and help in managing blood pressure.

Box Breathing

When having a panic attack, you can try box breathing as follows:

Inhale and count to 4

Hold and count to 4

Exhale and count to 4

Wait and count to 4

You can repeat these steps until you are in control again.

The reason this helps is that the slow expansion of your lungs can send signals to slow down your heart and this can help calm your entire body including your nervous system. The vagus nerve connects the signaling and releasing of acetylcholine which is a calming chemical that helps the body relax.

Remember the Cold?

Never forget that cold tunes the vagus response and this can slow down sympathetic nervous system activation. Cold exposure can help in relieving depression and anxiety. When you stimulate the vagal pathway, you also stimulate digestion. Cold exposure can reactivate the gastric nerves.

Take Care of Your Gut

Did you know that microorganisms in the digestive system communicate with the brain? The microbiome can be said to be the ecosystem of good bacteria present in your body and on your skin. Most times when people talk about this, they are referring to the microbes in the colon and intestines.

There have been studies on animal models as well as some human evidence that when the microbiome is thriving, it can boost mood and reduce anxiety. To determine if the vagus nerve was the reason for this, experiments were conducted on rodents with and without a vagus nerve. The ones with the vagus nerve seemed to experience reductions in anxiety as well as depression indicators unlike those without.

Developing Your Child

As a parent, you can help build the autonomic system of your child and tune their vagal pathways through loving care and bonding.

Giving your kids cold showers shouldn't be the first step as you should wait until they know that's what they want. During the infant stage, baby massages and skin to skin can help develop the baby's vagal tone. Once children are older, other ways to help tone their vagus nerve are cold blast showers and breathing techniques. Other ways to develop this include yoga, massage and mind-body techniques. The benefit of toning the vagus nerve is that it extends to the major organs in the body.

Surgically Implanted Electrical Vagus Nerve Stimulator

The vagus nerve can be activated surgically in order to more aggressively treat a dysfunction. There are surgical implants to stimulate the vagus nerve such as electric stimulators for patients who suffer from severe epilepsy or depression.

Find Your Safety Cues and Train Them

Finding your safety cues and training them with a little practice can help you feel safe. Your safety cues can keep your anxiety and fear responses from kicking in. A good way to go about this is finding your safe place or your happy place when you are calm. In order to do this, imagine you are in the place you feel most at ease and peaceful. Ensure to make use of sensory information as much as possible such as smells, sounds, and sights, and practice this visualization often. Then when you begin to experience fear or anger, you can initiate your safe place visualization with little effort.

Conclusion

Thanks to the polyvagal theory by Stephen Porges, there has been a greater understanding of how the human body works as well as how to help people in certain situations involving vagus nerve dysfunction.

The Porges' polyvagal theory was developed through his experiments with the vagus nerve. The vagus nerve can serve as the parasympathetic nervous system which is in charge of all the calming aspects of the nervous system. This parasympathetic branch of the autonomic nervous system can balance the active sympathetic branch in many more ways than was imagined before the polyvagal theory came along.

There are different ways to put this into practice which can help a number of issues such as depression, anxiety and even autism. It all depends on the vagus nerve, how it is treated, and how much it responds. Developing the autonomic nervous system is a good way to cope with many of the daily challenges we have as individuals.

Chapter Six: Using the Polyvagal Theory as a Counselor

Introduction

The polyvagal theory by Stephen Porges gives us a much better understanding of the nervous system. This theory helps us to see the nervous system beyond the two parts of the antagonistic system of which, one is stimulating while the other is calming. The theory brings to light the third kind of nervous system response which he calls the social engagement system, and this is a stage of being hyperactive.

He asserts that people in this stage have a mixture of activation, and calming only occurs with vagus nerve influence. Counselors are educated in the sympathetic, which is fight-or-flight, and parasympathetic, which is emotional shutting down or freezing, so counselors know how to help manage responses to life-threatening situations. The polyvagal theory gives us an understanding of how the branches of the vagus nerve can calm the body. Shutting down or freezing is caused by the dorsal branch of the vagus nerve. This reaction can cause fatigue (from being so stressed, especially felt in the muscles) and lightheadedness similar to that of the flu. If a shutting down of the system occurs, it causes people to automatically dissociate from others and disengage socially, preferring to be alone. At this point, they become moody and depressed. These reactions (caused by the ventral branch) can affect the lungs and heart, then affect the body beneath the diaphragm. Here, a lot of digestive issues arise. If there is unresolved trauma in our past, we might perpetually remain in fight-or-flight mode, increasing anxiety during our daily activities such as going to the gym, cleaning the house, taking care of the kids and doing well at work. Some may not be able to handle the trauma and in the long run, their system could destabilize.

How the Polyvagal Theory Helps a Counselor

The polyvagal theory is seen as the new science of safety. As a therapist in a clinical setting, you have to first test the person's autonomic nervous system before you help these patients by demonstrating and teaching self-help exercises. Stephen Porges' theory carries techniques that counselors need to help their clients or loved ones who are experiencing trauma (to move from trauma back to anxiety or activation mode). If people are found living their lives dissociating themselves, we must help them return from dissociation/immobilization to fight-or-flight mode; they need to be around people they trust to find a sense of safety. If they feel that they are safe with people, they can gradually socially engage.

There are two techniques to help people socially engage:

- CBT, or cognitive behavior therapy

- DBT, or dialectical behavior therapy.

One of the reasons why these therapies are very much appreciated is the amount of help they render to people who live isolated lives. They help by making people more conscious of their needs and the tensions they feel in their bones and muscles. Thus, people find it much easier to come out of the various traumas which they have experienced. It also helps them to deal with experiences that led to a shutdown of their senses.

Another concept these therapies teach is how to effectively deal with the various emotions you might be experiencing. Porges asserts that when it comes to taking action, the body already knows what to do before the mind catches up. An example of this would be the rape of a young woman. This unleashes a torrent of emotions. The outcome would likely be a shutdown of her emotions as she battles to deal with the shame that comes with it. The end result would often be dissociation.

To ensure that these sorts of emotional problems are addressed, many people today yearn to learn more about their body through the various therapies available.

Through these therapies, they can learn the ways in which their autonomic system works. They are then able to understand the intricate patterns which accompany traumatic experiences and emotional shutdowns.

There are a number of ways in which they can deal with this. The first recommended step is to write down how they feel. The truth is that people suffering from these issues find it difficult to express themselves. The key is to ensure they regain their ability to express themselves, no matter how long it takes.

Establishing Connection and Trust Between Counselor and Client

As a counselor, another way to do this is to have discussions that focus more on listening and learning how it all started in the first place. Counselors should make efforts to understand things exactly the way their patient sees and feels. This is the best way to help them solve the issues in their mind. One of the major keys to helping your clients is to exercise patience with them. They are going through a lot. Guiding them gently through this process will achieve much more than rushing them along the process. There is so much they don't understand and are facing, it is only fair that they are given time to come out of their dissociative behaviors.

Before the polyvagal theory, counselors were hardly taught to differentiate between the fight-or-flight response and shut down behaviors. They can now differentiate between defense responses for life-threatening situations and responses that characterize Porges' social engagement system.

It is important that counselors allot enough time to spend with their clients, without pushing the relationship of course which could have a negative effect. As a counselor, making sure that you are available whenever they need you will ensure that they maintain some form of connection even in their darkest hours. Allow the client to express problems they can't express to others, such as painful feelings and experiences, anger, and whatever else could be difficult to share with others.

According to the polyvagal theory, some people need to learn how to have trust-based relationships. Trust is built on feeling safe, and relationships are built on trust. This way, you feel safe and the sense of safety begins in the body. Even visualizing a physical connection with someone you feel safe with (your counselor, for example) can be helpful. Close your eyes and imagine that person holding your hands. Your heart rate increases when you imagine a physical connection as well as in reaction to real physical connection.

Remember that your thoughts are very powerful. If you

conclude within yourself that you cannot come out your state, it becomes difficult to do so.

Clients should be led to associate themselves with people whom they feel happy around.

Also, restorative surroundings have a special way of influencing the nervous system.

Clients should understand how their body reacts to stress so they can switch states. If they are in a dissociated state, they should follow the therapy guidelines to know how to pull themselves out of the disconnected state. Also, suggest that your clients use the self-help exercises discussed further on in this chapter.

Understanding the Ventral Nerve and How it Functions

One way in which counselors can help their patients is by using the ventral nerve. This nerve is often referred to as the engagement system because of the impact it has on certain parts of the ear. This ensures better hearing even in noisy areas as it filters out background noise. It also helps us read expressions and the patterns of facial muscles.

The ventral nerve also affects the larynx, amongst other body parts. The polyvagal theory asserts that most people facing issues of dissociation often block the world out as their inner ear would be dysfunctional. This is where counselors come into play. They help make sure that the vocal expressions along with the facial ones work together for appropriate messaging.

Breathing Techniques and Assessments

Familiarity with how the vagus system works is important. When people exhale slowly, the nervous system, particularly the parasympathetic system, is ignited. It is important then for counselors to ensure that their clients practice taking deep, slow breaths in and out on a regular basis.

Stanley Rosenberg suggests various methods that counselors can use to both establish a connection with their clients and better assess breathing patterns and vagal function. For example, he has suggested that the client should sit opposite the counselor.

Have the client open their mouth just wide enough to see their throat. When they make a sound, the normal action would be a contraction of the muscles in that region. The same effect is found when there is any form of swallowing. Sometimes, an additional response could be the popping of the ears. These sounds would allow the counselor to know just how free the client is and how to help them feel more relaxed. Check both sides of the muscles in the throat, namely the uvula and the soft palate, ensuring both sides of the muscles are lifted in the right proportions.

Another tool counselors can use to help their clients is diaphragmatic breathing (also known as belly breathing). Good diaphragmatic breathing is important for social engagement, and people in a state of stress have altered breathing patterns. As a counselor, you should be able to detect if there is a diaphragmatic issue by observing the lateral movement of the lower two ribs on both sides.

When inhaling, if there is a diaphragmatic issue, the body finds other ways to create space for the expansion of the lungs. The chest rises and expands in what is called chest breathing. This pattern of breathing is connected with emotions of fear, anxiety, and panic.

Some common examples of situations that might cause anxiety or fear include public speaking or performing on stage. Chest breathing may ensue, and you might feel the need to urinate, or your stomach might hurt. These are symptoms of stress in the vagus system. In situations like these that are not life-threatening, use vagal toning techniques: take long deep breaths, exhale slowly, try singing, keep a calm facial expression, and think of creative ways to begin. Remember that even if you make mistakes, we all make mistakes and are imperfect; we are all in the same boat.

COPD and Breathing

According to research, COPD (chronic obstructive

pulmonary disease) is one of the most non-communicable diseases in the world. COPD is caused by smoking or environmental pollutants as the body blocks airflow by laying down extra fibers in the lungs as a protective mechanism, causing the bronchioles to narrow. It is characterized by shortness of breath, poor passage of air and coughing. People with COPD find it difficult to breathe with any amount of physical activity. Inhalers, drugs and surgery are not the best answer here. Rosenberg's research using the polyvagal theory has been a success with COPD. The best course of action is to enroll in exercise training to improve lung capacity and increase the uptake of oxygen in the blood. Breathing can also improve by playing a wind instrument, playing drums, blowing balloons, chanting and singing.

Breathing and Hernias

With a hiatal hernia, the stomach protrudes through the diaphragm into the chest cavity, pushing into the lungs and making it difficult to breathe.

Have someone help you check if there is movement in your chest and belly when you breathe. Have them place their hands gently on the sides of the lower part of your ribcage to see if there is any movement in your lowest rib. If the diaphragm is functioning well, two lower ribs should push out and expand with each inhale.

Below are exercises that could help those with a hernia who find it difficult to breathe. They are basic exercises arranged in a specific order. Doing them lying down is best, but you could also recline in a chair or stand.

• Lie on your back, comfortably weaving your fingers of both hands together.

• Place your hands behind your head, resting the full weight of your head on your interwoven fingers. Your neck should be relaxed, not stiff.

• Move your eyes slowly to the right without turning your head, going only as far you can comfortably go.

• Count up to between 30-60 seconds, then exhale and inhale or yawn. This causes the autonomic nervous system to relax.

• Bring your eyes back to the center, looking straight up.

• Move your eyes to the left at this point.

• Practice the same thing by yawning or exhaling and inhaling. After you have done this you can check your breathing with the process described previously to see if your breathing has improved.

In addition to breathing difficulties, someone with a hiatal hernia likely also has acid reflux. This is when the stomach contents come up into the back of the throat (esophagus), causing heartburn. The shortened esophagus is a prime factor that can disrupt breathing. Treat with basic vagus exercises to lengthen and relax the esophagus.

Migraines and Muscle Tension

Problems with the trapezius and sternocleidomastoid (these are connected to spinal health) muscles cause severe discomfort such as pain, stiffness and migraines, and they are sometimes socially disengaged. Try this exercise:

Grab hold of the trapezius muscle on each side, massaging it lightly between your thumb and your first finger. Ensure the massaging is light because when you do this slowly, you are simply lifting the muscle slightly away from the underlying muscle. Both sides should be soft and supple, but sometimes one side could be soft and the other side tighter.

Neuro-Fascial Release

Rosenberg calls this next technique neuro-fascial release technique. With this, you should be used to doing massage with your hands.

- Lie on your stomach

- Try gently pushing the skin at the base of your skull (the occipital bone) to the right side, and sense with your hand the stiffness of the occipital bone.• Slide the skin to the left, again sensing the stiffness of the occipital bone.

•   Allow the skin to return to neutral.

•   Notice the direction which had more resistance, move slowly to the point of resistance and pause at that point. You can sigh, swallow or yawn. The resistance in the skin will dissolve as you release your fingers.

•   Once you test again, your skin should be easy to slide both to the left and the right.

•   Test your breathing again using the vagus nerve process mentioned earlier.

The Salamander Exercise

The salamander exercise improves flexibility and frees up the joints between the individual's ribs and sternum, resulting in increased breathing capacity. Having a straight head posture makes space in the upper chest needed for breathing. This exercise brings your head to the same point as the rest of the spine.

•   Put your head exactly at the same level of the spine.

•   Bend sideways to release muscular tension between your ribs and the spine. This increases the freedom of the movement of the ribs, which improves breathing.

Facial Expressions

Also, remember that facial expressions affect your nerves. Putting on a smile positively affects the cranial nerve, increasing blood circulation to the skin of the face and making one more lively.

• Stand in front of a mirror. Look especially at the skin on your cheekbones.

• A light touch on the skin and stimulates the end of the cranial nerve.

• Slide your fingers around your face and touch every part of your skin. Notice the part that has more resistance and hold that point until there is a release.

Other Activities that Enhance Vagal Stimulation and Support Proper Breathing

Engaging in physically difficult activities on a daily or weekly basis permits for building internal stamina which can keep one in fight-or-flight rather than moving into shut down.

Other activities that support vagal regulation include listening to music, engaging with friends and yoga classes. Combining social engagement with effective breathing is especially helpful.

Our understanding of the polyvagal theory can also help

make dance practices therapeutic. Dancing is a form of physical activity, improves your health, and you can start right away by enhancing your breathing.

Music, dance, and body movement shift one's psychological state. Components of music can be deconstructed into bio-behavioral processes like social engagement. Music improves vagal responses related to hearing human voices, especially singing with others and instruments such as violins, flutes, clarinets, trumpets, oboes, and French horns. This type of music helps us calm down, slows our heart rate, and our facial expressions relax as the sense of danger passes.

Conclusion

The polyvagal theory has had a global impact on both clients and counselors. Many counselors have used this theory to help improve people's lives. It helps us in facing the reality of life with many simple daily techniques such as putting on a smile, dancing out stress, singing, playing of instrument, having healthy thought patterns, being among positive people, knowing how to control your body and prevent it from entering into a state of trauma, and reaching out to a counselor, among others. These techniques can help anyone in any kind of distress. Based on this theory, Porges has been able to break down music therapy into behavioral processes to encourage social engagement and discover how clients react behaviorally and physiologically.

When calm, there is a physiological regulation in their behavior. We have also learned that a purposeful, mechanical change in our breathing has a calming, health-promoting effect on the vagus nerve. When through with this book, try to maintain a positive outlook. Don't ever say things like, "It will never work," or "I can't". When we change these thoughts, sooner or later you will appreciate this theory. Be on the lookout for neighbors who have similar problems to the ones mentioned here and show them these exercises; it could be a practical way to see how the polyvagal theory works. It is also important to keep records to see how it has changed your health.

Conclusion

So here we are, ladies and gentlemen!

If you have reached this point, a very big congratulations to you! You have proven yourself worthy of this path, and you deserve the very best that life has to offer.

Let's do a quick rundown of everything, shall we?

We started with the introduction of the nervous system. It was explained that the nervous system is comprised of two divisions: the central nervous system and the peripheral nervous system. The peripheral system is divided into two systems: the somatic nervous system and the autonomic system, and it was explained that the ANS is responsible for regulating the unconscious activities of the human body. The ANS is further divided into the parasympathetic nervous system, the sympathetic nervous system and the enteric nervous system, each with their own unique functions.

The sympathetic system regulates the homeostatic processes of the body and controls our fight-flight-freeze responses. When faced with life-threatening situations or stress, this system helps us to manage our responses. It helps prime the body for action, especially in life-or-death situations. It operates with the preganglionic and postganglionic neurons that send signals to different parts of the body to increase heart rate, promote blood flow to skeletal muscles and lungs, boost sweat excretion, constrict blood vessels to increase blood pressure, and improve far vision, among other effects. The outflow of the sympathetic nervous system is the thoracolumbar region of the spine.

The parasympathetic nervous system controls the body's unconscious functions while at rest. It is this system that controls lacrimation, salivation, digestion, urination, defecation, and sexual arousal. This system is otherwise known as the rest-and-digest system. It has a craniosacral outflow because of the way it is positioned and located. This system works with nerves that primarily emerge from these three sources: the cranial nerve, the vagus nerve and the pelvic splanchnic nerves. Some of the functions of the

PSNS include lowering heart rate, improving near vision, aiding sexual activity, promoting nutrient absorption and sexual arousal. These two divisions of the ANS, namely the SNS and PSNS, work in total opposition to one another, yet they greatly complement each other. Finally, the enteric nervous system is often referred to as the second brain, and understandably so. This system is responsible for controlling the function of the gastrointestinal tract. It acts independently of the brain and spinal cord but needs innervation from the sympathetic and parasympathetic nervous systems.

This brings us to the polyvagal theory. This theory was proposed by Dr. Stephen Porges in 1994, Director of the Brain-Body Center at the University of Chicago, Illinois. Porges created this theory after years of observation of neurology and evolutionary biology, and it shows that the ANS is linked to sensitive influences that run from the body to the brain (afferent influences). It states that humans have facial expressions that are linked to autonomic physical reactions such as digestive changes. It also links the relationship between the parasympathetic control of the heart, digestive tract and lungs, and our visceral experiences.

The vagus nerve is a component of the ANS, and this theory reveals that different branches of the vagus nerve produce different stress responses in mammals. It goes through a phylogenetic hierarchy, so we have the evolved branches and the primitive branches. The evolved branches coordinate social communication and behaviors while the primitive branches coordinate immobilization behaviors. Because of the hierarchy, the primitive branches do not come into play except in cases where the evolved branches fail. Note that the vagal system works opposite to the sympathetic-adrenal system (remember, the PSNS works in total opposition to the SNS).

How does this theory directly apply to us? Because we can understand and therefore influence vagal tone. The CNS responds to environmental stimuli to regulate homeostasis. When a person is subjected to stressful conditions, the rhythmic nature of the autonomic state is disrupted. The vagus nerve regulates heart rate in the parasympathetic nervous system via what is known as respiratory sinus arrhythmia (RSA). RSA is a normal phenomenon that causes an increase in heart rate upon inspiration and a decrease in heart rate upon exhale, with a difference of 15 bpm or greater considered normal. RSA, therefore, is used to measure the difference in stress reactivity, which makes vagal tone a good physiological indicator of stress.

Furthermore, we have Stanley Rosenberg's theory, a very relevant theory in the medical field. Rosenberg gives us practical insight into how you can access healing power from your vagus nerve. For people struggling with depression, anxiety, stress and other kinds of mental issues, Rosenberg reveals how the vagus nerve plays a strong role in how effectively you interact with other people. The vagus nerve is the longest in the ANS and is described as the tenth cranial nerve. This nerve sends out sensory fibers from your brain stem to your visceral organs. When a person is in a challenging, the nervous system discharges stress hormones such as cortisol and adrenaline into the body. Fainting, or vagal syncope, usually occurs when the vagus nerve is inconsistently stimulated while under stress, resulting in reduced blood flow to the brain.

Vagal tone is responsible for regulating the activity of the vagus nerve. The importance of Stanley Rosenberg's theory is that it brings to light the healing potential patients have within themselves. Patients that recognize this tend to heal faster.

This theory also emphasizes the importance of exercise for vagal stimulation. Furthermore, exercise sharpens your brain and helps improve your appearance.

The power of the vagus nerve also helps to reduce inflammation in the organs.

Finally, when vagal tone is high, feelings of happiness and joy increase. Who wouldn't want that?

Let's bring these concepts home. Statistics have shown that mental illness is one of the greatest causes of death globally. Many people are stressed at work, school and even in their homes, with no one to talk or relate to. How can these theories help people fighting trauma, depression, and even autism?

The normal functioning of the body is regulated by what Stephen Porges calls the social engagement system. This vagal system enables us to interact and communicate with other people from birth. But when we are stressed, it diminishes our ability to do so. Depression, like most mental disorders, is a malfunction of the autonomic nervous system. People suffering from depression have a sustained level of stress that keeps them unsettled and agitated. They feel a lack of motivation and drive, and their sleep is unrefreshing no matter how long it is. Normally, the vagus system uses the vagal brake to reduce the heart rate and stabilize the breathing patterns, but traumatic experiences impair the brake and leave the person in a state of imbalance. What can a person experiencing depression or trauma do in such a situation?

They should take advantage of breathing exercises. Since the vagus nerve is active when breathing is calm and the sympathetic system is active when breathing is fast, then short and shallow breaths tend to create a form of imbalance in the nervous system. Learning to change breathing habits by taking longer inhales to stretch the capacity of the lungs to take in more oxygen, and longer exhales for relaxation, can be very beneficial.

Autism is a disorder that affects a person's communication, interests, and social interactions. The polyvagal theory shows us that autistic individuals are unable to communicate, interact with people or analyze social data normally. As a result, their bodies often read fight-flight-freeze responses and shut down. During childhood, their body remains in immobilization mode. The consequence is that they become agitated, have difficulties digesting food, and their interactions with the outside community is distorted. Their social engagement system has not been fully integrated. This condition may occur as a result of emotional trauma, fear at birth, or their vagus nerve was silence or damaged, leading to their nervous system not fully developing.

So how does the polyvagal theory and Stanley Rosenberg's theory apply to them?

We are conditioned to think that our brains are fixed. However, research has shown that the brain can be rewired and reconditioned. It can activate new neural pathways and new neurons, thereby regenerating and stimulating areas that were not previously working properly. This field of study is known as neuroplasticity (brain plasticity).

There is therefore a beautiful ray of hope for autistic patients. Through various therapies and counseling sessions, people suffering from autism can learn to reconnect with their brain and body, gain mastery over it and above all, feel safe and secure in this beautiful world of ours.

The benefit of a well-stimulated vagus nerve is that you will be able to make great memories that will last a lifetime. The truth remains that with the development of the polyvagal theory and all the advancements which have been made thanks to this theory, the world has moved into one of the most promising eras of neuroscience and its related health issues.

Made in United States
Troutdale, OR
06/05/2024

20345523R00076